DEGREE COFFEE BY THE YARD

DEGREE COFFEE BY THE YARD

A SHORT BIOGRAPHY OF
MADRAS

÷

NIRMALA LAKSHMAN

ALEPH

ALEPH BOOK COMPANY
An independent publishing firm
promoted by *Rupa Publications India*

Published in 2013 by
Aleph Book Company
7/16 Ansari Road, Daryaganj
New Delhi 110002

Copyright © Nirmala Lakshman 2013

All rights reserved.

No part of this publication may be reproduced,
transmitted, or stored in a retrieval system, in
any form or by any means, without permission
in writing from Aleph Book Company.

ISBN: 978-93-82277-15-6

7 9 10 8 6

Typeset in Sabon Roman by SÜRYA, New Delhi

Printed in India

This book is sold subject to the condition that it shall not,
by way of trade or otherwise, be lent, resold, hired out,
or otherwise circulated without the publisher's prior consent
in any form of binding or cover other than that in which it is
published and without a similar condition including this
condition being imposed on the subsequent purchaser.

*To my great-grandfather Kasturi Ranga Iyengar
and my grandfather Kasturi Srinivasan who
made this city our family home, to my father
Srinivasan Parthasarathy who loved Madras,
and to my mother Menaka Parthasarathy
who gave us Chennai.*

*This book is also for Lila and Mallika in the hope
that even as they are citizens of the world,
Chennai will always anchor them.*

...But I know this city

                of casuarina and tart mango slices,
                gritty with salt and chilli
                and the truant sands of the Marina,

...

                the vast opera of the Bay of Bengal
                flambéed with sun,

and a language as intimate as the taste
of sarsaparilla pickle, the recipe lost,
the sour cadences as comforting
as home.

It's no use.
...Cities ratify
their connections with you
when you're looking the other way...

Arundhathi Subramaniam, 'Madras'

CONTENTS

Reflections of a Chennai Vasi 1

The Story of Madras 16

The Layered City 63

Of Performance and Spectacle 93

Chennai at Leisure 116

Degree Coffee by the Yard 133

In the End, the Beginning 141

Acknowledgements 147

Notes 152

Bibliography 157

REFLECTIONS OF A CHENNAI VASI

It's five in the morning on a nippy January day. An unusual drop in temperature does not deter the walkers on Marina Beach. It is still Madras at this time of the day, still the city of my childhood, and if I close my eyes for a minute, nothing exists between the sand, the sea and me. Dawn has already broken, and as the night's dark skies dissolve into silver, and a tremulous sun gathers strength for its usual vigorous passage across these southern skies, I see the walkers strung out across the sands: the Gujarati lady, unselfconscious in a violent yellow sari and walking shoes, the self-important businessman more intent on his mobile communication device than his prescribed exercise, and the little fisher boys who run the length of the Marina, their voices full of laughter. This morning, the more recent statues on the Marina remain a blur, so it is easy to pretend they are not there, and that it is still Madras as it once was, when there was only Gandhiji continuing forever on his lonely post by the quiet seaside.

There was no tiled pavement in those days, just the jagged sidewalk broken by pale yellow and burnt pink stone. You had to be careful not to step on the cracks in case someone you loved suddenly died. And then you had to skip down to the beach below to smell the salty sea spray. The sands were whiter then. If you looked back, you could see the sunlight bounce off the tall columns of the police headquarters and the statue of the lone policeman in his ludicrous khaki shorts and his preposterously tall hat standing to perennial attention. In the evenings, the balloon man would come, and along with him the man with the small handcart selling thenga-manga-pattani sundal, which we were of course not allowed to eat; but he would always hover temptingly around us, twisting old newspapers adeptly into conical containers. These things were our Madras.

Before the swell of morning walkers increases, one can easily imagine that the Marina is still the grand promenade dreamt up and built by Governor Grant Duff in 1884 to rival the best of those in Europe. Later, in the early decades of the twentieth century, the fires of freedom were set ablaze on it as hundreds of people thronged the beach to hear the passionate speeches of Bal Gangadhar Tilak and Bipin Chandra Pal against British rule. Gandhiji's Salt Satyagraha, paralleled by the Vedaranyam march in south India, had its echoes in Madras when the satyagrahis broke salt on the Marina. Today, this road is one of the few stretches that stands testimony to the continuity of history, despite the creeping kitsch of stainless steel railings and obtruding statues.

There is much in the Chennai (the name by which the

degree coffee by the yard

city has been known since 1996) of today that is still Madras. Orhan Pamuk, writing on Istanbul, his home of more than half a century, speaks of the spirit of that city and its stabbing beauty, its 'huzun'—a kind of communal melancholy and 'a way of looking at life that implicates us all...a state of mind that is ultimately as life-affirming as it is negating'. In recognizing this he pays homage to the splendours of an older civilization, the ruins and remains of which are visible everywhere in the city, overlaid though they are by a more dismal and confused modernity. Similarly, in Chennai, though there are no visible ruins, the spirit of old Madras leaps out of unexpected corners. It hovers in the smoke-filled mornings the day before Pongal, the festival of abundance, when the sun moves to the northern hemisphere and people filled with the resolve of new beginnings burn old rubbish in their houses; it exists in the still thriving kilijosiyam or soothsayer parrots who, with clipped wings and starved bodies, are trained at the behest of their owners to pick cards that will tell your fortune; you can see it in the eyes of young girls brightened by kohl or kan mai, their dark plaits thickly woven with fragrant jasmine strands. It rises from hot, freshly ground 'degree coffee' (an import from Kumbakonam) in roadside tea stalls, made with expert hand movements that draw the attention of passers-by. The echoes of old Madras also persist in the alleyways and streets of extended neighbourhoods, in small white houses with green louvered window shutters, and roofs ablaze with climbing red bougainvillea, hidden away behind ungainly concrete and steel buildings.

The best cricket is still played in historic Chepauk Stadium, where legendary players beginning with the great M. J. Gopalan once entranced crowds of frenetic cricket fans. Many of us have memories of afternoons spent in the pavilion, eating buffet lunches and watching the exploits of the men in white; most memorably the magnificent Garfield Sobers' smashing 95 runs on one never-to-be-forgotten occasion. Our real hero, though, was the dashing Nawab of Pataudi, whose elegant strokes we applauded with delight.

In December, the city's great traditions of art and music come alive, a tradition that began in the early twentieth century. From the august Music Academy to the more modest thatched roof halls, every year, both locals and outsiders, including non-resident Indians, get their fill of classical dance and music grounded in traditions that are centuries old. Along with symposiums discussing the intricacies of talam and tani avartanai—the rhythmic beat and the extended solos of expert musicians, connoisseurs savour a range of tiffin—medhu vadai and masala dosai being popular favourites. The mamis, with their diamond nose rings and silk saris, for once abandon their homes and the ubiquitous Tamil serials on television to savour the delights of the season, trading gossip as well as, in a more serious vein, discussing the poetry of Andal, the Vaishnavite woman saint, as expressed through *Tiruppavai* and critiquing the Bharatanatyam performances on display.

Growing up in the sixties and seventies, going to 'town' to find bargains in the wholesale markets was a

degree coffee by the yard

regular weekend activity for those of us who lived in South Madras. Finding unexpected treasures in the bookstalls of the now extinct Moore Market was one of the chief delights of a Saturday afternoon. Adjacent to Moore Market was Central Station, the pivotal point of travel of the city, from which we would make our annual holiday journey to the hills to escape the city's stifling summer. Beyond Central Station, in historic George Town (originally known as Black Town) with its maze of streets and localities, every neighbourhood remains a testament to the advent and contributions of various visitors and settlers in the city. Armenian Street, Mint Street, Coral Merchant Street, Sowcarpet and Popham's Broadway—the names conjure up the stories and images of travellers stumbling on to Madras's shores from as far away as Armenia and as close by as Gujarat and Rajasthan. They traded their wares and skills and found a warmth and friendliness among the local people that led many of them to settle here. George Town is also where the city's first commercial establishments took root.

It is possible for the discerning visitor to recognize that there are spaces and buildings in George Town that retain some of their original character; in the crumbling facade of buildings and in the charm of old street houses there is an unexpected poignancy. This was really once meant to be the heart of the city, yet today it seems to stand at the edge of the city's consciousness. Further north are Perambur, Vyasarpadi, Tondiarpet, Ennore and Tiruvottiyur, with their congested roads and railway settlements, gateways to the areas of darkness in North Madras. In these areas, the grime from factory smoke blackens the walls of dilapidated houses. Children with matted hair forage in piles of rubbish for food and other precious finds. Their parents toil for meagre daily wages in the wholesale markets, the industrial estates, the mills and small factories that crowd the landscape in this part of the city. This is also Madras, and yet it is another country.

÷

To the Chennai vasi (resident) of a certain age, Madras and Chennai seamlessly meld together. For some of us who grew up when Chennai was Madras, there was an obtruding awareness that, in Tamil, it was always Chennai, and hence there was an easy coexistence of nomenclature when we spoke of it. This was because the anglicization of the family did not dilute our strong Tamil heritage and the name Chennai was never far from our consciousness. It could be argued, nevertheless, as the historian A. R. Venkatachalapathy points out, that a kind of 'colonial' echo revolves around the term 'Madras', while the 'unsung yet glorious' aspects of the city are very much alive in the more broad-based vernacular vision of Chennai.

Whichever way you have it, this is a city that has an uninterrupted flow from the past into the present. The name 'Madras' is now a repository of not just colonial memory, of the actual origins of a city, but also the name of a place that was a physical reality for most people of a certain generation. In other words, to state a rather self-evident truth, this is a place where we were children, and also where we became adults. 'Chennai', as another appellation of the city, has existed since the founding of Madras in the seventeenth century, and was the name used commonly by Tamil and Telugu speakers. Even though 'Chennai' became the official name of the city in 1996, in assertion of a wider vernacular identity, the name 'Madras' still represents the time preceding this period in many people's minds. However, as memory, history and politics are diverse and often contested spaces, there can be no rigid interpretation of what the name 'Madras' now stands for. It remains mostly a term reflective of a certain affectionate nostalgia nursed by people habituated to the appellation, even though they themselves are unlikely to use it in regular parlance.

To actually feel a city like Chennai the senses have to be extended. Its pulse can be gleaned as much from the nine-yard saris still worn by orthodox Brahmin women drawing their kolams (the intricate patterns drawn with rice flour that adorn the entrances of many homes signalling auspiciousness) in the Brahmin quarter by the temple, as from the keerakari, the greens seller, who markets her astonishing range of spinach with indefatigable gusto and the pookari, the flower vendor, whose basket of jasmine and marigold assaults the senses. The spirit of the city also hovers in the bylanes of Triplicane, where amidst crowded dwellings and the flurry of daily commerce, it is possible to stumble unexpectedly into serene courtyards of old mosques offering a retreat into quietude and prayer for the local Muslim population.

The city's essence is likewise visible in the traditional Nadar kadai, or provision stores, that are the lifelines of neighbourhoods and run by the Nadars, an enterprising community who came to the city from southern India. In modern Chennai, many Nadars have climbed to positions of success as politicians (including a chief minister), media barons, film stars and captains of industry; and few have forgotten the city that nourished them. Similarly, another traditional community from the deep south, the Chettiars, many of whom began as financiers and made their fortunes in Burma and Malaysia, came back to the city to redraw its contours through a range of contributions. From setting up manufacturing industries in sugar, fertilizers, steel tubes and bicycles to the enriching and preserving of traditional Chettiar art and culture clearly visible in many of their homes, the city stands testimony to their contributions. It is the confluence of such traditions that have shaped the modern city.

Chennai's spirit is also visible in a certain modern *Tamilness* that is worn with pride. Madrasis are not just the 'idli-vada-sambar' lot (as some outsiders like to call them) although idli-*vadai*-sambar continues to be a breakfast staple in homes and eating places. A T-shirt company (which manufactures T-shirts with messages like *Peace, Love and Filter Coffee*) proclaims on its website: 'Our lives have shifted from veshtis to

Bermudas, pavadai-dhavani to kurthis', but 'we love to preserve our culture in a trendy way'. Despite the obvious commercial intent, the message is also about a new sense of the city—one that is visibly modern yet rooted in tradition. This tradition is not a homogenized tradition but composed of diverse strands, springing from history, memory and cultural practices spread across dissimilar inhabitants.

The notion that Chennai is *more* traditional than other Indian cities seems to persist and is often used as a convenient tag line to describe the city. While this is a bit of an exaggeration, it is unquestionable that tradition endures, but is usually recast and incorporated into a more modern and global idiom. For instance, young English-speaking college-going men of Chennai will often call each other 'macchi' which is really a traditional but slangy Tamil abbreviation for 'brother-in-law', but which is now widely used even by sophisticated speakers to emphasize their linguistic affinities. A modern Chennai woman will unhesitatingly swing her handbag against a rowdy at the bus stop who hollers 'whatte figure' at her, and curse him roundly in 'Tanglish'. She will also hang around her grandmother's kitchen trying to learn the secrets of brewing the perfect filter coffee. 'Two carefully measured spoons of freshly ground beans...okay-va?' the grandmother might say. This blend of tradition and modernity manifests itself wherever you look. For instance, there is a group called Hip Hop Tamizha, a band of rappers whose youthful exuberance has caught the imagination of many young people. Their compositions reflect the aspirations and lifestyles of not just young men, but also recognize the free spirit of modern Tamil women, albeit in a slightly sexist way at times. The Kolaveri song, sometimes considered an extension of the city's gana tradition (a distinctly urban form of folk music originating from the city's slums), is another example of modern Tamil sentiment transcending local boundaries, although after a short-lived viral life it seems to have disappeared into oblivion. It does, however, encapsulate the modern Tamil youth's keenness to bring a distinct local idiom into a transnational musical rhythm. The new inventiveness in the use of language and the clever adaptations of old traditions and identities into a newer construct is what gives modern Chennai one of its most defining characteristics.

This book hopes to pull together a sense of the city from lives that have been fashioned by it. Like most cities, migrations within and from outside have defined its character, and its many labyrinths of culture, politics, perceptions and identities resemble those of other modern conurbations. But Chennai is also defined by the uniqueness of its story, and the memorable moments that have nurtured its people, its institutions and its way of life. As I traversed its streets and engaged with its people, I found that there were probably as many iterations of the Chennai story as there were people to tell it. What was common to a significant percentage of the people I met was how much these people cared for the city. Even when there was a sense of dismay or disappointment with the way it was, there was nevertheless a proprietary sense that indicated a deep personal involvement with the city. There were however poignant exceptions to this. To some of the people I met, the notion of the city simply had no meaning. They live on its fringes, and are frequently swept aside by its callous civic apparatus which cares little for them and makes little or no effort to lift them out of the poverty they are mired in. The story of the city is also the story of these people—the many who laboured to build it but were not able to find a space of their own within it. These are people who have been edged out of their original places but continue to work to sustain the city's economic progress. They are the construction workers, the brick layers, the small vendors, the Corporation workers and the daily wage labourers whose services and hard work keeps the city afloat, although they themselves are often choked by its brutish apparatus.

÷

In his remarkable tribute to New York City, E. B. White described the city as a 'goal', a 'final destination' for those who come 'in quest of something'; this was what gave it 'its incomparable achievements'. As with White's New York, so is it with Chennai. As that indefatigable chronicler of the city S. Muthiah points out during one of our conversations, most of the residents of Chennai do come from elsewhere, from their 'ooru' or 'place' (be it town or village), in search of better opportunities, despite frequent warnings about the city bringing one to ruin, and it is they who keep its vitality and passion alive. Muthiah himself comes from a prominent Chettinad family. He lived and worked as a journalist in Sri Lanka before settling in Chennai where his parents were. A prolific writer who has written more than thirty books on the city such as *Madras Discovered* and *Madras Rediscovered*, and writes a column in *The Hindu*—'Madras Miscellany' (begun in 1999, which has also been compiled into a book)—Muthiah's is the final word on the city's colonial heritage. With a private tabloid called *Madras Musings* and through the annual Madras Week celebrations, Muthiah has, more than most people in the city, rallied its citizens to the cause of heritage and conservation. As a mentor and friend, I owe much in this book to the long conversations I was privileged to have with him as we sat and talked in the beautiful lounge of the Madras Club, evocative of the era when the city actually came into being.

Interestingly, as Muthiah tells me, even when families have been in the city for a couple of generations, they still have strong connections to their places of origin. It is not uncommon, as I have often noticed, within a few minutes of introduction to a person, to be asked in that peculiar Tamil brand of English, 'And yoou-er native?'

My own 'native', which I have rediscovered in recent years (having always thought of myself as a Madrasi, or Chennai vasi as I should perhaps now call myself) is the small village of Innambur nestling between the green paddy fields and the coconut groves of the Kaveri

degree coffee by the yard

belt in Thanjavur district just three miles from the temple town of Kumbakonam known then as 'the Cambridge of south India'. This was largely because of the multitude of clever mathematicians that the region produced. My great-grandfather, Kasturi Ranga Iyengar, was no mathematician but a conscientious, if not brilliant student, who after primary schooling in Innambur village went to the Provincial School in Kumbakonam and was then sent by his father to Presidency College in Chennai (which was situated in Nungambakkam in those days) to do an arts degree. After obtaining his degree in 1879 and completing a brief stint as a Sub Registrar in government employment, he passed the bar in 1884 and moved to Coimbatore to practice as a lawyer. Although Kasturi Ranga was described as 'being of a shy and retiring disposition' and somewhat hesitant in speech, it obviously did not hinder his interest in politics and public affairs. Before he moved to Coimbatore he was a founder member of the Madras Mahajana Sabha which became a forum for the expression of public opinion and the development of political consciousness in the Madras Presidency. The offices of this forum were in the premises of the newspaper, *The Hindu*, started by six young nationalists in 1878 with the goal of public service. When Kasturi Ranga returned to practice in Madras in 1894, he resumed his association with this forum and also took a leading role in the activities of the Indian National Congress, which met in Madras in 1898 and again in 1903. Meanwhile, he became *The Hindu*'s legal adviser in 1895, and when the paper, which had by then become one of the leading voices of nationalist politics and sentiment in the Madras Presidency (albeit recognizing some good aspects of the Empire's rule and influence) ran into financial difficulties just after its silver jubilee celebrations, Kasturi Ranga bought it for seventy-five thousand rupees, much against the advice of many friends and well-wishers. Obviously he made the right decision. One hundred and thirty-five years later, *The Hindu* is thriving in the city of its origin and is respected nationally for its credibility and authenticity. It is still the paper that the majority of the city's inhabitants turn to for the morning news along with their first cup of coffee. Speaking of coffee, although *The Hindu*'s connection with Chennai's favourite beverage remains a deeply rooted image, coffee itself as a daily fix for Tamilians and the people of Chennai became fashionable only in the late nineteenth century, according to the historian A. R. Venkatachalapathy. In his delightful essay in the book *In Those Days There Was No Coffee*, he points out that coffee began its journey as a drink of the Europeans; however 'by the turn of the twentieth century...coffee had captured the imagination of the middle class, which ultimately appropriated it to suit its goals'. Venkatachalapathy closes his exploration of the state's coffee drinking habit by quoting the writer R. K. Narayan: 'I never tire of writing about coffee. It seems to me an inexhaustible, monumental theme. I sometimes feel that it is a subject which may well occupy the space of a whole saga...'

degree coffee by the yard

One of the things this book will dwell on is the coffee or filter kaapi phenomenon. It will also delve into the history and memory of Chennai, the way we were, the way we are now, our culture, our institutions and monuments, our music and dance, our food and our literature, the pain and the pleasure of our ordinary lives, and how the many become one, distinct yet together, within the purlieus of the great city.

THE STORY OF MADRAS

The tale of this city is really one of two cities—Madras and Chennai. Let's look at each of them by turn—Madras in this chapter and Chennai in the succeeding one. Madras grew out of the small British settlement of Fort St George in the seventeenth century, and echoes of it were still palpable when I was a child, and continued as I grew into adulthood. The Chennai of today is a big, sprawling metropolis, complex and layered, in which old Madras can only be glimpsed every now and again amidst the trappings of a twenty-first-century city.

The footprint of the city is very old in some parts. Archaeological digs conducted by the British geologist Robert Bruce Foote in 1863 and 1864 in Chennai suburbs like Pallavaram and Attirampakkam revealed a hand axe (the first discovery of an Old Stone Age tool in the entire Indian subcontinent) followed by the discovery of a number of other tools of the same era, indicating the presence of people of the Stone Age. Iron Age implements found in Guindy, now very much in the heart of Chennai, also point to the antiquity of the region in which the city now stands. Professor K. V.

Raman, historian and former head of the Department of Archaeology and Ancient History, Madras University, who has documented the early history of the region in great detail, has pointed out that a small sarcophagus, burial urns, and iron implements unearthed, astonishingly enough, in the garden of a private residence on Hall's Road, Egmore, are evidence of the presence of early man in this region. Obviously the terrain with its rivers and rocks was highly conducive to the life of early man. What is perhaps most interesting about the region is that archaeologists and historians both affirm the continuous presence of human beings in the area since the Palaeolithic Age. If we leap forward a million years or so, Roman coins and painted pots found in areas like Egmore, Kilpauk, Chetpet and Mambalam are a sign that there were flourishing communities and people living in the region who were involved in trade with lands across the seas. In fact, the town of Mylapore was known even to the Greek geographer and astronomer Ptolemy (who lived at the end of the first century CE and into the second century CE) and figures in his writings as 'Mylarphon'.

The ancient Tamil dynasties of Chola, Chera and Pandya are mentioned on the Pillars of the Emperor Ashoka (273-232 BCE), not as a part of Ashoka's empire but as separate kingdoms that had existed in the south for at least a hundred years before the Pillar inscriptions.

The period between the third century BCE and the third and fourth century CE is largely shrouded in the mists of time. Literature of the Sangam Age speaks of

Tondaimandalam as the region of the future Madras/ Chennai and its surroundings, and mentions the names of various local chieftains who held sway, such as Ilam Tiraiyan, who may or may not have been a representative of the family of the early Chola rulers referred to on Ashoka's Pillars. After this time, until about 600 CE, the entire region was under the Kalabhras, who overthrew the existing Tamil kings and captured their territory. In time, the Pallava dynasty of kings came to power and controlled most of the Tamil country, overthrowing some minor Chola kings and driving out the Pandyas who were rulers further in the south (there was a revival of Chola rule some centuries later). The finest examples of Pallava art are the rock-cut temples of Mamallapuram (Mahabalipuram), now about sixty kilometres from the city. Built around the sixth and seventh centuries, these marvellous structures on the shores of the Bay of Bengal are a must-see for visitors who come to Chennai.

THE TEMPLE OF THE LILY TANK

In Chennai itself, the Parthasarathy Swamy Temple in Tiruvallikeni (now Triplicane) stands out as one of the near-perfect symbols of the city and the region's antiquity dating back to the Pallava period. Tiruvallikeni acquired its name from 'keni', meaning sacred tank, and 'alli', which means lilies in the midst of a forest of tulsi. This area is probably the oldest part of the city with historical continuity from roughly the fifth or sixth century CE onwards. The Mudhal Alwars or the first Vaishnavite saints who lived in the fifth and sixth centuries visited this temple and composed songs in praise of the deity. One such composition by Peyalwar, one of these early poet saints, describes in evocative verse the coral and pearl deposits from the sea illumining the entire village of Tiruvallikeni. A composition by another poet-saint called Budattalvar of the same era describes the shrines in detail and also describes the ecstasy of just being in the temple. The temple tank, filled with lilies in the days of yore, was in itself held in great reverence. The father of the Vaishnavite philosopher Ramanuja was advised to bathe in it as he and his wife were childless. The story goes that soon after he bathed in the tank a child was born to him. The child, of course, grew up to be a great reformer-scholar of Hinduism. The town that grew around the lily tank was ultimately named after it.

Tirumangai Alwar, whose presence dates back to the eighth century, also visited the temple. Curiously, in his compositions he clubs this temple and Tiruvallikeni with 'Mayilai' (Mylapore) and there are inferences that there was a strong connection between the two neighbouring towns even at that time. It appears that much of the description of the temple and shrines in the works of all these poets reflects what exists in the temple today. The historian Dr Chithra Madhavan tells me that an inscription in the temple corroborates what Tirumangai Alwar wrote in the thirteenth hymn, *Periya Thirumozhi*. She says, 'It mentions that the temple was built by a chief of Tondiayar, a Pallava king, whose name, however, is not on the inscription. This proves that the Tiruvallikeni temple has been in existence in one form or another since Pallava times.'

Interestingly, there appear to be two entrances to the temple, but as Chithra explains to me, originally there were two temples back to back, each with a main deity, its own rituals and processional events reflecting traditions of worship that are centuries old. This temple, like the one in Thiruvidanthai, another hoary temple just outside the city on the East Coast Road, is considered one of the 108 holy shrines of Vishnu. The other curious aspect that Chithra mentions, one that is not found in many temples, is the number of deities positioned in the main sanctum. The main deity is Lord Krishna (called Venkatakrishnan or Parthasarathy) and is surrounded not just by his consort Rukmini, but also his brother Balarama, his son Pradyumna, grandson Aniruddha and the warrior Satyaki. Krishna, as the epic hero Arjuna's charioteer, is expounding the truths of existence to Arjuna and pointing to the way of enlightenment through knowledge and detached action or karma yoga as described in the Bhagavad Gita. The grand demeanour of the main idol draws devotees from across the city. I wonder if the Tamil penchant for sporting moustaches emanated from here, as the handsome deity sports a splendid specimen (this is the only Vishnu temple where the deity has a moustache).

Since many of the Alwars have composed songs about the temple and its deities with great elaboration, historians like K. V. Raman suggest that it must have existed many years before their time. Interestingly, some of these poems, as Dr Raman points out, also describe the surrounding areas—one verse suggests that the place was full of storied buildings, inhabited by women of exemplary character. Other verses speak of gardens, ramparts and pavilions. Obviously, at least in the eighth and ninth centuries, Tiruvallikeni was much more than a village.

÷

From the same era as the Tiruvallikeni temple, but relocated and rebuilt several times, is the Kapaliswarar Temple in Mylapore, another very significant temple for Hindus. It is mentioned in the *Thevaram*, a collection of poetic compositions of the seventh-century Saivite saints such as Tirugnanasambandar and Appar. It is likely that the temple was first constructed over two thousand years ago, although it has been subject to periodic renovation even as recently as within the last three hundred years. There are beautiful tales and legends associated with the temple; one such is the seventh-century tale of the girl Poompavai, who was supposedly raised from the dead by the saint Tirugnanasambandar, who sang her back to life by his worship of Kapaliswara and his appeal to the deity. S. Muthiah, that tireless chronicler of the city, quotes a lovely verse (loosely translated) from the saint's plea in his book *Madras Rediscovered*:

Where are you Poompavai?
Lord Kapaliswara has chosen beautiful Mylapore as his seat
Surrounded by sweet smelling punnai trees
Why hast thou gone without seeing
The legions of the Lord given their repast here?

The dancer and writer Lakshmi Viswanathan, who has a vast repertoire of stories about the city and the region, reminds me of the ending of the tale of Poompavai. After she is brought back to life, Poomapavai's father asks the young saint to marry her. Caught in a quandary, he finds an apt answer. He cannot marry her as he gave her life, he says, and is therefore like a father to her. Lakshmi tells me that the story of Poompavai is re-enacted very elaborately at a temple festival every year. The punnai tree in the outer courtyard of the temple is, according to Muthiah, one of the few left in Mylapore today, and this particular tree is said to be one of the oldest in Chennai.

S. Anvar, a soft-spoken documentary filmmaker, writer, and photographer who is currently researching Tamil Muslims, points out that early Buddhists and Jains also lived in Mylapore where these faiths initially flourished and coexisted. (Mylapore was also known as Mayura Sabda Pattinam, so named by a Buddhist scholar-monk.) But, in time, fearing persecution, many are likely to have converted to Islam, as they did elsewhere in the Tamil country.

Centuries later, the temple tank of the Kapaliswara shrine was built on land gifted by the Nawab of the

Carnatic, and even now Muslims are allowed use of the tank on Muharram day. This kind of simple amity between communities is a hallmark of the city's syncretism, and a quiet symbol of its steadfast secularism.

÷

In the first few decades of the Common Era, around 52 CE, St Thomas, the Apostle of Christ, is said to have landed on the shores adjacent to Mylapore, and preached on the beach which later came to be called San Thome by the Portuguese, who built a settlement there. Legend has it that he was buried here on the coast of Madras around 72 CE. There are all sorts of theories about the saint's visit and his martyrdom, one of which actually refutes the notion that he visited San Thome. No matter, for each sceptic, there are dozens of true believers! Marco Polo's account mentions a little town in India where 'the body of Messer Saint Thomas the Apostle lies in this town...having no great population. It is a place where few traders go... Both Christians and Saracens frequent it in pilgrimage...' Marco Polo refers to another narrative of the times which suggests that St Thomas was accidentally killed by the arrow of a fowler who had aimed at peacocks, for which the area was well known. The reference may have been to Mylapore. Later on, other travellers from Europe, particularly Portugal, came to investigate the death of St Thomas. One of these, Gaspar Correa came from Portugal in 1521 and wrote that he found an ancient church in 'Mayilapur' with crosses and peacocks as 'decoration'.

÷

To go back to the ancient kingdoms and dynasties of the region, the Pallava rulers were in control of the entire area from the second to the ninth century CE with the historic town of Kanchipuram as their capital. Then came the great Chola kings whose dynasty flourished up until the fourteenth century, and whose headquarters were further to the south in Thanjavur. Among the Chola rulers, the greatest was Rajaraja Chola (947-1014 CE), who was followed by his son Rajendra. The builder of the magnificent Brihadeeswara Temple in his capital Thanjavur, Rajaraja was also a great empire builder and a patron of the arts. Stories about the king abound, and I remember one that my mother used to tell me when I was a little girl. Apparently, people of a certain stature in society were always accompanied by a little boy who would carry a small box of betel leaves and nuts for their chewing pleasure. The master sculptor of the Brihadeeswara Temple employed a boy for this purpose so that he could continue his great work even as he reached out for his betel nut and leaves. The story goes that this man was so absorbed in his work that he raised his hands with palms outstretched behind his back wanting the boy to press his palm with the much needed sustenance. It turned out that the boy had temporarily vanished from the scene but someone stepped up behind the sculptor and pressed his palm with betel leaves. The sculptor who was absorbed in his work did not look back right away, but when he did, he saw that it was the king himself. Such was the respect that Rajaraja accorded to artisans and craftsmen that he did not hesitate to temporarily humble himself in the face of great genius.

The Chola kings extended their empire through conquest all the way up to the north of India. The Siva temple in Gangaikondacholapuram commemorates the extent of Rajaraja's son Rajendra's kingdom which went as far north as the Ganga and down south to include Sri Lanka. The boundaries of his kingdom were said to have extended up to Burma; Thailand and the Khmer kingdom of Cambodia were his feudatories. Apart from developing military might and naval power, the Chola kings built schools and temples and encouraged economic activity around these temples. They also promoted art and literature. The dynasty went into decline at the beginning of the thirteenth century when the Pandyas rose to power. After a hundred years or so the Pandya rule weakened, having been eaten away by smaller rebel chieftains and kings, following which the generals of the Delhi Sultan Alauddin Khilji overthrew them, establishing a Sultanate that extended as far south as Madurai.

At the end of the fourteenth century, the dynasty from Vijayanagar, Karnataka, conquered most of south India and ruled this vast territory through local governors who were called Nayaks. Of the parts of the territory that did not belong to them, there were some around the future Madras that belonged to the Nawabs of the Carnatic. These areas had devolved on the Nawabs after the decline of the Mughal Empire and were ultimately annexed by the British. When the Portuguese arrived on these shores to trade in 1522, as mentioned earlier, they built St Thomas's Basilica and also a port called Sao Tome after St Thomas. In the mid-1500s, they also built Luz Church, the oldest surviving church in the city today. The story goes that a group of Jesuit friars (some legends say sailors) from Portugal, whose ship was lost on the rough seas and about to sink, prayed to Mother Mary. They soon saw a mysterious light that led them to shore and safety. In gratitude for their safe arrival they built the Church of Our Lady of Light—Nossa Senhora da Luz. Locally it was called 'kaattu kovil' meaning jungle church; obviously it was in the midst of a dense forest.

JOHN COMPANY FINDS A PLOT

And thus we come to the British, who were the actual founders of the city of Madras. Its physical origins began around 1639 when Francis Day, a hard-drinking, womanizing English trader of the East India Company, and his superior Andrew Cogan, who were based in Machilipatnam, accepted the grant of a strip of land from the local Nayak chieftain, Damarla Venkatadri and his brother. The strip was on the sandy Coromandel Coast near the fishing village of Madrasapatnam. The grant was intended to expand trade in the hinterland that offered 'excellent long cloath and better cheape by twenty per cent than anywhere else'.

The historian S. Muthiah tells me that originally Fort St George (as the settlement was called after the patron saint of England, St George) comprised just a warehouse for the traders with a couple of armed guards to protect it. The area around Fort St George was named Chennapatnam after the father of the Nayaks, Chennakesava Nayak, who was also a relative of the Raja of Chandragiri. The dual name of the soon-to-be city has therefore existed from the time of its inception.

There has been much speculation about the origin of the name 'Madras'. In Col. Love's *Vestiges of Old Madras*, he records that the land was acquired from a fisherman called Madrasen. Another theory suggests that the name came from a wealthy Portuguese family called Madra. The origin of the name has also been attributed to the presence of madrasas in the area, but this is the least likely theory as the area was only occupied by a few fishing villages and was more likely to have been under the influence of the Portuguese in nearby San Thome.

The architect P. T. Krishnan points out that when Fort St George was built, it was modelled on forts built in Wales and certain other parts of England, which had sea gates (small gates opening into the sea) with the forts facing inland. The sea gate was necessary to ensure that armaments and other defences could be procured via the sea (in case of an attack). It seemed a bit strange, though, that Madras would need to be well-fortified, as it was meant only to be a trading port; but then the British were far-seeing and keen to protect their ventures from military aggression. Sure enough, Fort St George was soon to experience attacks by marauders owing allegiance to the Sultan of Golconda.

More than a hundred years later, all the fortified buildings in the complex would also withstand attacks by the French, although adjacent Black Town was captured and destroyed. The British resolutely won everything back and indeed went on to expand their turf as John Company (as the East India Company was colloquially called) made way for the Empire. The Fort became the citadel of British administration in India, long before the Crown acquired Bombay or founded the city of Calcutta. It was the first Corporation to be granted a seal by the British East India Company in 1687.

WHERE MODERN INDIA BEGAN

The Fort complex houses the state government's Secretariat and the State Legislative Assembly. It is ironic that the once colonial centre of power should still serve as the focal point of the state's administration. However, this is where Madras began, and a visit to the Fort reveals much of the story of John Company, a company that came to trade and stayed to build a great empire, which became the jewel in the crown of England.

As I step into beautiful St Mary's Church across the

path from the main Secretariat building and the Legislative Assembly, I find a silence and serenity that is in welcome contrast to the disturbing presence of government functionaries swarming outside. Built in 1680, the church is the oldest British church in the city, and thought to be 'the first Protestant church east of the Mediterranean Sea'. It was built during the governorship of Streynsham Master, and was possibly designed by the Fort's gunner, William Dixon. Many famous men of the time were married here, including Elihu Yale and Robert Clive. As I wander its quiet precincts, I imagine the pomp and circumstance this quiet little corner of Madras must have witnessed in its time; the Governor in his fine regalia coming to worship with family members in tow, guards in attendance, all slowly making their way down the aisle towards their pews. The beautiful wooden fretwork behind the pulpit and on the balustrades contrasts strikingly with the simplicity of other parts of the church. On the floors and walls are tablets in marble and stone dedicated to the memory of those who served the Company and the Crown, including some of them in a humble capacity. Interestingly, the font was donated by Job Charnock who served at the Fort and later founded Calcutta. The rock from which the font was made is known as charnockite, found only in Pallavaram, on the outskirts of the city.

There are other significant buildings in the complex, including Fort House, The Exchange Building (which is now the Fort Museum), the King's Barracks and

Admiralty House (which is known as Clive's Building and home of the office of the Archaeological Survey of India). It took a couple of decades to complete the Fort complex including the Fort itself, which took thirteen years. The streets were given grand names like Charles Street, James Street and Gloucester Street; soon the area became known as 'White Town', with English, Portuguese and Armenian officers, administrators, soldiers and families living there. In time, an outer wall was built to shelter the increasing white population. Just beyond, and to the north, lay 'Black Town', where local traders, artisans and other natives who served the needs of White Town lived. Interestingly, the country's first mint, first school, first hospital and first Town Hall came up here, which is why Madras chroniclers correctly claim that the origins of the modern Indian state began in this city. Barring the three years between 1746 and 1749, during which the French attacked and captured Madras, the British always held sway here, slowly adding villages beyond Black Town to their territory.

Neeti Anil Kumar, who is Assistant Archaeologist of the Fort Museum, shows me the sloping green knoll on the banks of the moat that the ASI has built so the Fort resembles the original structure constructed by the British. We peer from the bank into the moat below. 'At one time, the British inhabitants of the Fort even used to fish here,' she says. Although it did not look like there could be fish in the shallow water of the moat, it is a considerable improvement on the garbage-strewn ditch that it was a few years ago. 'Now we have a beautiful garden that runs on all sides of the moat,' she says proudly. 'We have been severely restricted in our functioning because much of this is under the army, and a lot of it is with the state government,' she adds.

'In so many ways everything began here,' Neeti says. 'What you see today in modern India, whether it is hospitals, nursing, schooling, or administrative services, everything began here in this very fort. In 1640 they [the British] founded the first mint the minute they entered. They didn't have any minting rights but they went ahead anyway and used the images of their king and queen. The French and Dutch, however, got permission from the local rulers to make coins. They even minted them with images of Indian gods and goddesses. Mughal coins were in currency because it was Mughal rule all over the country. The British minted their own coins and when the Mughal emperor Aurangzeb came to suspect this and intended to put an end to it, the British quickly withdrew all the coins in circulation so he didn't find anything wrong. If he had, he would have stalled the British perhaps and maybe the history of India would have been different,' she says with a smile.

At this point we are joined by K. Moortheeswari, the Deputy Superintending Archaeologist of the Fort Museum. The archaeologists show me around the rooms where the exhibits range from coins of pre-colonial days, such as those from Tipu Sultan's period to those of the Company and the Raj. Other rooms contain suits of armour, rifles, bayonets and various armaments. There is also a nineteenth-century military petard, a wooden device from which small bombs were launched, and the ladies are pleased to elaborate on their knowledge of the Shakespearean phrase 'hoist by one's own petard'. They show me how the contraption could accidentally blow up the person who planned to use it against an enemy.

I see the rare porcelain used at the table of the nawabs and also those of prominent Europeans of the times. Moortheeswari also shows me the various tasting dishes that were used, made of fine bone china, delicately hand-painted, some of them with coats of arms. 'The servants had to taste the first mouthful from all this fine china in case there was some poisoning attempt by enemies. At least they got to taste good food for all the service they did,' she quips. What I found most admirable about Moortheeswari was her fierce but humorous anti-colonial frame of mind; despite being soaked in the historicity of the Fort and even proud of all the artefacts that have been preserved, and are in her charge, it is refreshing that she can see the British in India for what they were.

As we pass a large marble statue of the third governor-general of India, Lord Cornwallis, at the foot of a grand wooden staircase, she says, 'Please examine the carving at the base of this statue that shows the defeated Tipu Sultan handing over his young children as hostages. Now, is this what this man wanted to celebrate when he ordered a statute of himself?' She remarks on how

Cornwallis had organized a huge parade to celebrate his statue's arrival in Madras; as it was taken by in procession, he is said to have saluted his own statue. 'Many of these fellows did not prosper in their country and came here, made money and went back to success and fame. We obviously had the art of turning failures into successful people. We made people great. Even that fellow Clive, who began his life here as a mediocre clerk, tried to commit suicide twice when he was in service in India. He managed to do it only the third time when he had gone back to England. We did the British a world of good,' she says with great emphasis.

Robert Clive would go on to become one of the Empire's shining lights and the architect of British power in India after his modest beginnings in Fort St George. Although perhaps no more corrupt and unscrupulous than others, when he faced a parliamentary committee that was investigating charges of corruption against him, during his later years in England, he famously remarked, '…I stand astonished at my own moderation', meaning he didn't really enrich himself as much as he could have.

GEORGE TOWN—THE FIRST HUB OF MADRAS

To the north of the Fort was the original Black Town which later became George Town, in honour of George V's accession to the throne as the King-Emperor of India in May 1910. One Sunday morning, V. Sriram, Sushila Ravindranath and I set out for a whistle-stop tour of George Town. An engineer who runs his own business, Sriram is a passionate raconteur of all things Madras, especially its heritage. Like Muthiah, Sriram is generous about sharing his time and information. Sushila is a friend of many decades, a fellow journalist and our families, like many others in Chennai, are connected in multiple ways. On the beach road, as the line of colonial buildings comes into view, Sriram explains they were built in the Indo-Saracenic style, an amalgam of Victorian neo-classical, Scottish baronial and Italian, mixed with elements of Indian Mughal and even Malabar style, an aesthetic pioneered by Robert Chisholm, the engineer who built them. The Senate buildings, parts of the Chepauk Palace, (now housing university departments) the General Post Office, Victoria Public Hall and some other smaller buildings are all his work. Chisholm was a rival of Lutyens who hated the Indo-Saracenic style, Sriram tells me, but his views found favour with the viceroy, Lord Hardinge, which is why Rashtrapati Bhavan in Delhi is built in this style.

We stop at the point where Black Town/George Town starts. Across the wide road are two small hamlets, originally Muthialpet and Peddanaickenpet (they still carry the names), which were not part of the town, Sriram tells us. 'This was where the dubashes [interpreters, those who spoke two languages–"do bhasha"] lived, as well as the devadasis, the moneylenders and the first weavers. We all know Francis Day found that cloth produced here was much cheaper than anywhere else, and so this was the entire business of Fort St George.'

Sriram pinpoints the exact moment in time when Madras came into being. 'The Nayak of Poonamallee, Damarla Venkatadri, just like the chief ministers of today, gave the British a tax concession for cloth trade. The Dutch were also in competition here and had the same dubash, Malayappa Chetty. There's a street here named after him. Madras began here but had just about four people—Andrew Cogan, Francis Day, Beri Thimmappa (Francis Day's agent) and Naga Battan (a gunpowder maker for the East India Company) while nearby San Thome, three miles down the road, was really the big city then and had five thousand people. Incidentally, Portuguese San Thome was considered the White Town, like the one in Fort St George; that is, it was the place where the white population lived, and Mylapore where the local people lived, served as the Black Town. We know of course that the village of Mylapore had been flourishing for centuries before that,' he adds. Pausing at the Law College complex, Sriram explains that this was called the Guava Garden and was the burial ground for hundreds of the British who died because of illness and war, many of them young. 'When the French took over Madras for three years between 1746 and 1749, parts of Black Town were razed. When the British later regained the territory, they decided not to build on the huge open space between Black Town and the hamlets beyond, as they felt that it was the presence of Black Town, with a large civilian population, that had prevented them from mounting a suitable defence against the French. There were thirteen pillars marking the boundary, and it was called the Esplanade when it was built. Now the road adjacent to this is called Esplanade, but originally the Esplanade was a huge expanse of empty land for defence and for clear fire towards the sea.' Most of the tombstones were taken back into Fort St George when the space was cleared, except for the tombs of Elihu Yale's son David and the Powney vault of the Powney family, whose members served at the Fort garrison. The Yale tomb is still here, says Sriram, but as Elihu had many 'chinna veedus' (or 'small houses')—the famous Tamil euphemism for mistresses or concubines; Yale had at least three, each with her own establishment—one is never quite sure whose tomb it really is. The present High Court was built here in the 1890s, the only building in Madras city that has its own pin code, other than the Indian Institute of Technology (IIT) Madras. The Armenians (Armenian Street is named for this community) were merchants who came to trade and were the right hand of the British. They were renowned for their honesty and loyalty. Sriram tells us that when the French laid siege to the British garrison in the eighteenth century, the leader of the Armenians, Khojah Petrus Voskan, who was the wealthiest man in Madras at that point, refused to go over to the French side and offered them money instead. The British were delighted with this, so when they returned they further strengthened their bonds with him. St Matthias Church in Vepery was built by Khojah Petrus Voskan and he is buried there.

degree coffee by the yard

The graceful Armenian Church in George Town that we later visit has cool courtyards, isolated frangipani trees and hushed noiseless interiors. It seems evocative of the Armenian community's simple integrity and the values they stood by even though they amassed fortunes and were enormously successful; especially in Madras, a place that they more or less co-founded. Although the community has completely disappeared in the city, there are Armenians in other parts of India, says Sriram, and they continue to maintain the church in George Town.

We drive by St Mary's Higher Secondary school, the oldest girls' school in the city; next to it is St Mary's Co-Cathedral, one of the oldest churches in British India built in 1658 by the Capuchins, a Franciscan order. Nearby is St Antony's Church which is also very old and especially popular with Hindus who flock there on Tuesdays to light candles.

I am struck by how so many of this city's people set aside the narrowness of the religious conventions they were born into to embrace a wider way of being. The use of a place of worship like St Antony's Church by communities other than Christians is a testament to this way of living. Sriram remarks that a lot of the early concerts of the Tamil Isai Sangam were held here, as when it was first set up in 1941 to challenge the stranglehold of the Brahminical Music Academy on Carnatic music, it had no venue in which to hold its performances. Many Carnatic musicians like M. K. Thyagaraja Bhagavathar, K. B. Sundarambal and

M. S. Subbulakshmi would sing of the glories of Lord Muruga in St Antony's Church. 'Nobody objected, and that was real secularism,' Sriram points out, adding that at one M. S. Subbulakshmi concert three thousand people gathered in the streets around the church to listen to her. Another strikingly beautiful historic building in this area is Annie Besant's Gokhale Hall, built in 1914. Inside the now derelict space one can see a breathtakingly beautiful oratory hall where both Mahatma Gandhi and Jawaharlal Nehru once gave speeches. 'Annie Besant set up the Young Men's Indian Association (YMIA) here,' says Sriram, adding that this was also the first home of the freedom movement in the city, as patriots gathered here regularly to meet and strategize.

As we drive by slowly, we see parts of the old town wall that still remain. Built in the late 1700s by Paul Benfield to protect the city from attacks, there is now a terraced garden positioned above the remaining portions of the wall called maadi poonga, or 'the upstairs garden'.

Sriram then tells us how, in the eighteenth century, beyond Broadway, between Muthialpet and Peddanaickenpet was a large open gutter through which the sewerage of the city flowed out to the sea. In the late 1770s, Sriram says, 'a visionary lawyer called Stephen Popham came to Madras from Calcutta, saw this gutter and announced "I am buying this ditch", which of course evoked great merriment all around.' Popham, who soon became an alderman, fought to establish a police service, wanted all streets to be named and to have lighting. But he remained silent on the real estate he had bought. At an opportune time, Popham pointed out to English generals like Eyre Coote how the hillock beyond called Narimedu or Hog's Hill had to be removed as it had proved to be advantageous to invaders like the French who could train their guns on George Town below. Everyone at once saw the wisdom of Popham's suggestion. But where could they put the earth that had to be removed? 'In Popham's ditch of course!' says Sriram. The ditch thus became valuable real estate and the vast expanse called Popham's Broadway became a place to which many of the English soon moved, as the Fort had become too congested. Sriram points out that the first cinema theatre was built here, as was Harrison's of Broadway, one of the city's oldest catering places. Venkatachalam's Ice, one of the city's first private ice-making facilities and many other small businesses of Madras first began in this area.

THE GOVERNORS CONSOLIDATE POWER

Madras grew steadily after Day and Cogan set up the first settlement in Madrasapatnam, (the adjacent settlement was called Chennapatnam) thanks to the efforts of Day's dubash Beri Thimappa as villages around the Fort slowly became part of the expanding city. Triplicane was the first village to be added on an annual rent of a hundred and seventy-five rupees from the Sultan of Golconda in 1676. When the Golconda dynasty ended, the paying of rent also came to an end and Triplicane was fully annexed in 1720. In 1693, Egmore, Purasawalkam and Tondiarpet were acquired by the East India Company and in 1703 five more villages including Nungambakkam, Tiruvottiyur and Vyasarpadi became part of British territory.

As the city grew, fortunes were made, often by disreputable means. One of the agents who represented the company, Edward Winter, who made a fortune through private trade, also created a small rebellion in Madras when George Foxcroft, another agent, tried to suspend him. Later on, Foxcroft was appointed the first governor of Madras. Foxcroft himself was accused of many misdeeds, and in addition, as Muthiah describes in his book, *Madras Rediscovered*, he was forced to write to the Company's directors in England about how to deal with a murder. The murder was committed by the wife of a Councillor, Mrs Ascentia Dawes, who killed her slave girl, Chequa. This triggered instructions from England about how to conduct a trial by jury and the first trial by English law was held, although with a less than satisfactory outcome as the lady who 'murthered' was pronounced 'not guilty'. While the slave girl may not have got justice, the first implementation of British ideas of law and justice was seen.

The governors who followed Foxcroft included notables like Streynsham Master, who was said to have been a great lover of pomp and was the first to introduce government records and rules for administration. When Elihu Yale became governor in 1687, the British

Government took over the territory from the Company, and in 1688 the Madras Corporation was established. It boasted a mayor and became the first structured administration of British India. Madras Corporation is therefore the oldest of any city in India. Long before Yale's casual donation (from wealth acquired in Madras) to a faraway college in Connecticut, America, where his name was immortalized by that distinguished educational institution, he spent many eventful and turbulent years in Madras consolidating the presence of the British in India and repulsing invasions by the Mughals and the Marathas. A few years and a few governors later, the French, who were constantly at war with the British over territory in India, apart from their ongoing conflicts in Europe, captured Madras and destroyed Black Town as well as the village of Chepauk and then took the Fort. In 1749, the British regained control of the lands they had lost and strengthened the Fort against subsequent attacks. Robert Clive, who arrived in India as a young soldier and displayed great military prowess as he led battles in Arcot and Trichinopoly, was among the first to re-enter Madras after the French defeat.

Following victories in other battles in the south, the British gradually drove out other European contenders from the region. They also defeated Hyder Ali of Mysore, and later his son Tipu Sultan; in course of time they achieved complete control of most of south India. Meanwhile, the city of Madras grew with administrative reforms. As the harbour developed, trade increased, with merchants like Thomas Parry arriving from England in the late eighteenth century and setting up his mercantile company. He later established a partnership with John William Dare, another merchant. (Dare House still exists and Parry's Corner is very much a part of the city's lexicon.) Parry's enterprise, EID Parry, which is now in the hands of the Murugappa Group, is the oldest surviving mercantile company in India. Other companies like Binny and Co., (which later closed down) Gordon Woodroffe, Spencer's, (tragically burnt down in a fire in 1983) as well as Arbuthnot and Co., were all set up during this period of consolidation of British power and commerce.

÷

The Nawabs of Arcot initially represented the Mughal Empire; in 1690, the Mughal emperor Aurangzeb appointed Zulfikar Ali Khan his man in the Carnatic and charged him with wresting the land from the Marathas. It was during this time, when Governor Yale was in charge, that the English quickly got new grants from the Nawab for Egmore, Tondiarpet and Purasawalkam and added to the territory of Madras. S. Anvar says that Ali Khan's successor, Nawab Dawood Khan 'threatened the safety of Madras from San Thome' and frequently demanded the return of villages granted to the British only to be bought over by the shrewdness of officials like Governor Thomas Pitt, who sent the Nawab 'four hundred bottles of Liquors'. Many of the later Nawabs (however able and enlightened some of them were) faced trouble from the British, until they were disenfranchised if they did not produce any heirs under Lord Dalhousie's infamous nineteenth-century Doctrine of Lapse.

Special mention must be made of Nawab Muhammad Ali who was given the title of Wallajah by his overlord, Emperor Shah Alam. He was extraordinarily generous in terms of donations to temples and churches as well as to mosques. The Kapaliswarar Temple's tank was dug on land donated by him; he gave elephants to many temples, and to St Mary's Church in Fort St George, he presented a painting of *The Last Supper*. While Wallajah could be unpredictable and devious, he was also known to be charming and hospitable. It was said that he loved all things European and even took to eating breakfast and lunch sitting on chairs as opposed to cushions on floors. The lovely Wallajah Mosque in Triplicane, known as the Big Mosque, was built by him in 1749. When I visited the mosque with my friend Anvar, he showed me the beautiful engraved chronogram made by Rajah Makkan Lal Khirad, a non-Muslim. Anvar points out that nowhere else in the world is there a mosque with a chronogram by a non-Muslim.

I was struck by the austere beauty of the Wallajah Mosque—its cool marble and granite expanse that could house so many of the faithful who came to pray; soaking in the stillness, the morning silence, I was moved by this city of many faiths, with its minarets, domes, spires and gopurams which had nourished the prayers and hopes of so many of its inhabitants.

÷

Through the years Madras was ruled by a succession of governors, some of whom were somewhat enlightened like Trevelyan and others who were very popular like Thomas Munro. (His mounted statue at one end of Mount Road is a favourite of many Madras children of a certain generation. There is a lovely story about a little English boy who lived in the city and who would drive with his father every day to see the statue; when his father told him one evening that he would have to say goodbye to the statue as they were leaving for England, the little boy asked, 'And what is the name of that man on Munro?') Soon, the British administration in the city and its surrounding areas became the Madras Presidency by the provisions of the Pitt India Act. However, it was only in 1858, a year after the First War of Independence (once known as the Sepoy Mutiny) that all of British India came directly under the rule of the Crown by order of Queen Victoria.

At this time, the city had a motley population of Telugu, Tamil, Kannada and Malayalam-speaking residents. People were excited by the city's infrastructural growth; many of the new arterial roads such as Mount Road connected two ends of the city. Easy movement of people and goods was facilitated by the building of new roadways, railways (the oldest railway station in British India was in Royapuram), bridges and navigable waterways. Buckingham Canal was a man-made waterway meant for navigation and trade, constructed in the nineteenth century. Although it is now navigable only in some places, Chennai's distinguished novelist, essayist and critic Asokamitran recalls how even as recently as the 1930s and 1940s, when he was a young boy, he used to watch boats laden with bales of hay, sacks of grain, fresh vegetables and other goods ply up and down the canal just behind Thanithurai Market in Mylapore. Now, behind the crowded market, the only reminder that the canal was once such a waterway, is a lone water lily that struggles through the slush and the small dark pools of water that stagnate between the rocks on the canal bed. Asokamitran tells me that Madame Blavatsky and Colonel Olcott, the founders of the Theosophical Movement (headquartered in Madras) often used the waterways, going all the way up to Nellore in rowing boats with singing boatmen.

While the British were busy consolidating their positions in the Presidency and elsewhere in India, two great famines broke out, one between 1876 and 1878 and again between 1896 and 1897. Thousands died in the Presidency as well as in the city of Madras where, like in other parts, diseases, particularly malaria, coupled with starvation, caused deaths running into several millions.

A GROWING DISCONTENT

The appalling attitude of the British administration, whose repressive policies and skewed trade practices had led to the famine in the first place, and the meagre relief that they made available to the victims, fuelled growing resentment towards the rulers and led to much ferment and discontent in the region. Englishmen like A. O. Hume, who were deeply unsettled by the policies of the government, helped set up (along with others) the Indian National Congress which would become the cornerstone of the long struggle to oust the British.

As a sense of nationalism slowly began to stir across the country, in Bengal as well as in Madras and Bombay, activists began to propagate their views by forming social and political organizations, and establishing newspapers to give voice to their collective views. In the early days of the freedom struggle, many important activists and contributors were from Madras. The Madras Native Association, a political organization, was set up by Gazulu Lakshminarasu Chetty in 1852; he also started a patriotic newspaper called *The Crescent*. This was followed by the establishment of the Madras Mahajana Sabha whose members were largely drawn from the politically-conscious intelligentsia. Newly established newspapers like *Swadesamitran* echoed the growing call for freedom. *The Hindu*, founded in 1878 by six young patriotic men, two schoolmasters and four law students all in their twenties, with little capital and no experience, soon became an important forum for voicing public opinion and grievances against the foreign rulers.

The third session of the Indian National Congress, which, by the late nineteenth century, was a power to reckon with, was held in Madras in Mackay's Garden off Graeme's Road in 1887. It was historic because of the election of Badruddin Tyabji, the first Muslim President of the body, and was a resounding success with several hundreds of delegates attending. *The Hindu* lauded the appointment of the Muslim President. It commented: 'Considering what power the co-operation of the Mahomedans will impart to the Congress, the Hindus may even go to the length of offering a promise to respect the scruples that the whole Mahomedan community as represented by their delegates may entertain...'

A singular and striking voice that catalysed the social, political and literary landscape of Madras and indeed later the rest of the nation was that of one of India's greatest poets—Subramania Bharathi. As the freedom movement began to gain momentum in the early years of the twentieth century, Subramania Bharathi who was born in Tirunelveli district in 1882 and lived for long periods in Madras, greatly stirred the imagination of the Tamil people. He infused the first two decades of the twentieth century not just with his patriotic fervour and the great beauty of his poetry, but by his imaginings of a freedom that was much greater than political liberation—the freedom of the mind and the freedom from fear. Often compared to Shakespeare, the range and depth of his poetry and writings demonstrated an unusual genius. He wrote about many things: about birds and children, about love and fearlessness, and about the land and its beauty. He also wrote odes to

Tilak and Gandhi (whom he admired and met once) and about courage and conviction. Bharathi was more than a poet and visionary. He was a journalist, an activist, a freedom fighter and social reformer who passionately believed in a just society, the emancipation of women and spoke out against social orthodoxy. He was a revolutionary whose association with Tilak, Aurobindo, V. O. C. Pillai and other freedom fighters led to the British trying to arrest him. He spent some years in exile in Pondicherry and was finally jailed by the British. Much of his writing was also banned.

My maternal grandfather, V. Bhuvaharan—who was drawn like so many of his generation to the freedom movement—a Gandhian who went to jail a couple of times, was a great admirer of Bharathi. My mother and her siblings learned all his poems; she remembers that my grandfather was particularly fond of the feminist ones, especially the one about Bharathi's vision of the new Indian woman, which no doubt my grandfather wanted all his daughters to emulate.

> Nimirndha nannadaiyum nerkonda paarvaiyum
> Nilatthil yarukkum anja nerigalum

This loosely translates to 'an upright walk, a steadfast, direct gaze, and eyes that are afraid of nothing on this earth', and was a particular favourite of my grandfather's.

I found a charming first person account of the great poet, written by a ninety-seven-year old friend and neighbour of his, N. Ramaswami Iyer, when he lived in Thambu Chetty Street around 1920-1921. Among many other things, the writer recounts a memorable incident.

degree coffee by the yard

'It was salary day. Bharathi arrived from the office in a rickshaw and told his wife that he had gifted [sic] his entire pay packet to the rickshaw-puller "since his need was greater than ours". She was shocked, because it was she who would have to contend with the monthly bills. Greatly agitated, she voiced her problem to us. I felt I should do something. A friend and I met the rickshaw-puller and explained the situation. Moved to tears, the poor man returned Rs. 45 (he had spent Rs. 5 on buying food for his starving family). Was not Bharathi the humanist who sang "The crow and the sparrow are of our clan and the oceans and the mountains our agglomeration"?' The old writer concludes that his memories of Bharathi are his most precious possessions.

The great humanist poet connected unusually to everything and everyone around him. There is another oft-told tale like the one above, which reveals his extraordinary generosity. His loving but long-suffering wife found him one day scattering the meagre amount of rice that they had left in the household to the birds outside. When she remonstrated with him, he pointed with delight to the birds that flew in to peck and feed on the scattered grain.

One day in June 1921, as was his regular practice, Subramania Bharathi went to the Parthasarathy Temple in Triplicane (where he lived) to feed the temple elephant. Suddenly, the elephant, whom he had befriended, turned rogue and attacked him. Already worn out and fragile, with years of hard living behind him, the poet never recovered from this. He passed away in September 1921 at the age of 39.

At that time, in Madras, there were multiple forums that rallied to the nationalist call of Bharathi and others. The esoteric group, The Theosophical Society, founded by Madam Blavatsky and Colonel Olcott in America, moved to Madras and established themselves in Adyar, where, among their spiritual and occult explorations, they also studied eastern religions and preached universal brotherhood. Though not directly involved in the freedom struggle, they contributed to the Indian cultural and spiritual renaissance and urged social reform. One of their brightest stars was the brilliant Annie Besant, the Irish rebel who was passionate about the idea of freedom for India and organized the Home Rule League in 1916, advocating Dominion status for India in the empire. She was President of the Indian National Congress at one time, and although neither Mahatma Gandhi nor Nehru quite agreed with her views, they admired her spirit and passion. (Annie Besant also famously 'discovered' Jiddu Krishnamurti, a young boy who had been living in Adyar with his brother and father, and proclaimed him as the future 'World Teacher'. He went on to become an internationally renowned philosopher.)

COUNTERING CASTE HIERARCHIES

1916 also saw the emergence of the Non-Brahmin Movement in the Madras Presidency. This was led by P. Theagaraya Chetty, Dr T. M. Nair and others to advance the social, economic and political cause of non-Brahmins in the Presidency as a counter to Brahmin dominance in public life. Caste issues and conflicts, a canker in Indian society, had persisted since the early formation of the city. Even in the seventeenth century, soon after Black Town was created, there were conflicts between the so-called 'right hand' castes and 'left hand' castes. For instance, the Chettys were considered to be left-hand, and the Komattis and Vellalars were right-hand castes. Initially, these disputes were related to modes of worship, the use of certain streets of Black Town and social strictures. However, as many castes began to rise up the social ladder through education and commerce, they began to question the place of Brahmins at the top of civil society; one of the areas that they focused on was the dominance of Brahmins in top positions in government. For example, in 1855, 237 of the highest posts in government were held by Brahmins out of an available 305 positions. The Justice Party was set up by Theagaraya Chetty and T. M. Nair who met at the Cosmopolitan Club, and as A. R. Venkatachalapathy wrote, drafted 'the manifesto that laid the foundation for the first organized non-Brahmin movement in India'. It was the culmination of anti-Brahmin sentiment; the party participated in the diarchy form of administration in the Madras Presidency after the Montagu-Chelmsford Reforms, which saw the British yield some ground on power-sharing in government. The party won the first ever direct elections in British-ruled India in 1920 and became the alternative to the more nationalist Congress party. When Periyar

E. V. Ramasamy took over the reins of party leadership, he also initiated the Self-Respect Movement, which focused on the notion of self-respect and freedom from the sense of inferiority imposed on certain castes by the Brahminical order; he felt this fight for equality was of critical importance, perhaps even more so than freedom from British rule. As much as he criticized the Brahmins, Periyar also criticized Hinduism and Hindu superstitions in periodicals like *Viduthalai* and *Justice*. Although, in time, the party's political clout would dwindle, it was the origin of the two dominant present-day Dravidian parties who have alternately held power since the Congress was routed in the state of Tamil Nadu in 1967.

The winds of freedom having blown through Madras, particularly after Mahatma Gandhi's campaigns, many were also inspired to join Congress and begin working for social and political reform in the country. In Madras, prominent lawyers like S. Satyamurthi, S. Srinivasa Iyengar and Chakravarthi Rajagopalachari (or Rajaji as he was known) plunged into the freedom movement. When Gandhiji made his first visit to Madras in April 1915, accompanied by Kasturba, he was given a rousing reception at Central Station the likes of which 'had been equalled in few instances before' according to *The Hindu*. The report added, 'Long before the arrival of the Delhi Express, the station platform and the compound had been filled in its strictest sense with people who had come to welcome Mr and Mrs Gandhi... When the train arrived, they searched all the first and second class compartments but in vain... A long search discovered Mr and Mrs Gandhi sitting in the third class compartment.'

Madras's connection with Gandhiji was special in many ways, not the least of which was the fact that his son Devdas married Lakshmi, the daughter of his friend and fellow freedom fighter, Rajaji. Gopalkrishna Gandhi, former Governor of Bengal, writer and essayist, and the grandson of both Gandhi and Rajaji, recounted to me the story of one of Gandhi's visits to the city: 'My mother once told me that after Gandhi had come and stayed with them in Madras, there was a complete transformation of the family; they were not the same again although at that time my mother was very young. But her elder sister, my aunt, recalled that Gandhi and she had a very fine conversation, an extended conversation long before my mother had any connection with him. This was in 1919, on one of his early visits to Madras. Gandhi was invited to stay in Kasturi Ranga Iyengar's house by Rajaji.

'Gandhiji and my aunt Namagiri, who was then something like eight or nine, had long conversations which had nothing to do with politics and nothing to do with Rajaji. He asked her about what she liked to read, which books were her favourites, and when she spoke to him it was in English. He was very admiring of this young girl's English and told her, "You speak as good English as the girls I've known in South Africa". So my aunt was very chuffed. But what was most important was what he himself describes as an epiphany.

In the twilight hour between sleep and consciousness, he said, the idea of an all-India hartal occurred to him. So the original idea, which he fleshed out later, actually came to him under that roof, under Kasturi Ranga Iyengar's roof. It was a remarkable thing and after that everything changed.'

÷

It must be mentioned at this point that historians like A. R. Venkatachalapathy have rightly argued that in the history of Madras, too little space is given to political movements other than the Indian nationalist movement. However as he says in his book *Chennai Not Madras*: 'The history of Chennai draws attention to them. The labour movement played a very important formative role in the making of modern Chennai (the oldest organized trade union in India was the Madras Labour Union founded in 1918).'

When the Indian National Congress first won limited power in the 1937 elections in the Madras Presidency, Chakravarthi Rajagopalachari became the first chief minister. He legislated the Temple Entry Act which stipulated that no castes should be denied entry to temples, and also called for the compulsory introduction of Hindi in schools, a measure that was very unpopular. There was a widespread anti-Hindi agitation that was a precursor to those that came later.

T. Prakasam became chief minister after World War II with the support of K. Kamaraj of the Congress party, and when India became independent and the Madras Presidency became Madras State, O. P. Ramaswamy Reddiyar became the first chief minister of Madras in the new nation.

In the 1952 elections, C. Rajagopalachari was again appointed chief minister of Madras as the leader of the single largest party that won the elections, although the Communist Party of India had put together a majority through a coalition of several parties. The long-festering demand for the linguistic division of states intensified during this period along with the demand that Madras become a part of the proposed Andhra state. The Madras Mannade (Madras is ours) movement gathered momentum with the support of leaders like T. Prakasam and others who wanted Madras to be the capital of Andhra. Prime Minister Jawaharlal Nehru fiercely resisted the demand for a separate state, and a freedom fighter, Potti Sriramulu, a Telugu born in Madras, went on an indefinite fast to protest the Prime Minister's stand. In December 1952, after fifty-seven days of fasting, Potti Sriramulu died; immediately there was widespread violence and fears for the safety of Tamils in Telugu-dominated regions. The demand was finally acceded to with the Wanchoo Report convincing Nehru and others about the genuine need for a separate Andhra state without including the city of Madras in it. A. R. Venkatachalapathy wrote: 'Despite the seeming controversy, the Andhra demand for Madras was a rather sectarian one... What gave impetus and nationwide visibility to the agitation was that it was linked to a very popular, genuine, and long-standing demand for a separate Telugu-speaking province of Andhra. But in fact the demand for Madras unnecessarily delayed the formation of this province. The relative quiet with which Tamil Nadu responded to the Telugu demand for Madras was rooted in the certainty that it was most obviously a Tamil city...'

A NEW STATE ASSERTS ITS IDENTITY

K. Kamaraj was already a politician of national eminence, and a name to be reckoned with in the Congress party before he became chief minister of Madras in 1954. He began life in Virudhunagar, a town to the south of Chennai, and his father, who belonged to the Nadar community, was a coconut merchant. When Kamaraj's father died, his mother sold all her jewels to support the family. Although the young boy dropped out of school and worked in his uncle's shop, he was idealistic and principled. News of the Jallianwala Bagh massacre shocked him; he plunged, even as a young boy, into the freedom struggle and participated in Gandhiji's Non-cooperation Movement as well as the Vaikom Satyagraha. He became a Congress party worker and was subsequently imprisoned six times by the British. He spent a total of nine years in jail.

After Independence, the political leadership in the State of Madras was dominated by Brahmins, but Kamaraj quickly rose to the top of the party echelons because of his simplicity and integrity. His presence as a Congress leader drew a lot of politically-minded non-Brahmins to the party, as many people had resented Brahmin dominance in the state. In 1954, when he became chief minister, he surprised everyone by appointing two of his rivals, M. Bhaktavatsalam and C. Subramaniam, to his Cabinet. A simple man who never forgot his humble beginnings, power meant little to him. He was, however, an able administrator who created primary schools in every village and high schools in every panchayat. He was the first chief minister to introduce the concept of the midday meal scheme in rural schools and just as he did much for literacy and education, he also helped farmers with irrigation schemes and encouraged the growth of industry in the state.

After Kamaraj, who introduced a host of popular measures in the state, M. Bhaktavatsalam became chief minister. The adoption of Hindi as the national language (a hotly debated issue even with the framers of the Indian Constitution) and its imposition in the south was bitterly opposed by the Dravidian parties, and the switching over to Hindi as the sole official language in 1965 sparked agitation and riots across the state. Students in the city who marched from Napier's Park to the Secretariat in Fort St George to submit a petition to the chief minister were further incensed when he refused to meet them. C. N. Annadurai, the leader of the Dravida Munnetra Kazhagam (DMK) was arrested; rioting and arson spread rapidly. The anti-Hindi agitation died down only after states were given assurances that they could transact officially in the language of their choice including English.

MADRAS INTO TAMIL NADU

One fallout of the attempt to impose Hindi on the state was the people's growing disillusionment with the Congress party. In the state elections in 1967, the DMK came to power, and C. N. Annadurai became chief minister for a brief period before his unexpected death from cancer in February 1969. One of the first things that his government did was rename the state. Madras became 'Tamil Nadu' (land of the Tamils). Annadurai introduced the popular one rupee per measure as the cost of rice, and also legalized the 'suyamaryathai' or 'self-respect weddings' which obviated the need for an officiating Brahmin priest (as had been the custom until then). The new government emphasized non-religious, secular functioning, and planned to push economic and social development at all levels of society. It also valorized Tamil and Tamil culture. Streets were renamed for Tamil heroes including those who lost their lives in the anti-Hindi agitation.

A. Srivathsan points out in his essay in *Chennai Not Madras* that even as the Dravidian parties had seized on the notion of a secular, non-elitist, non-casteist ideal of Tamil society (exemplified even in Sangam literature), they 'intelligently and dexterously used different methods to mobilize an idea of distinctive identity'. Films, literature and architecture were the tools of this mobilization. He says that physical spaces which were under the control of the state were deftly used to reinforce the glories of Tamil culture. Thirteen statues of Tamil literary figures were built on the Marina. Buildings like Poompuhar were constructed in the city to commemorate *Silapathikaram*, a great Tamil epic. In Kodambakkam, the building of Valluvar Kottam, a memorial to the great Tamil poet Thiruvalluvar, was begun when the DMK first came to power to serve as a public hall, (the auditorium can seat 4,000 people) a research centre and a place for learning. For all its secular identity, traditional 'stapathis' (sculptors specializing in temple carvings and sculptures) were used to build it, and its design draws much from temple architecture, including the use of the Thiruvarur Temple car from the hometown of DMK party leader Karunanidhi. Although the construction of Valluvar Kottam was interrupted because of the national Emergency declared by Prime Minister Indira Gandhi and had to be completed later, it is a memorial that clearly reasserts Tamil identity. Currently, although it is a public monument, it is used as a venue for various exhibitions.

After Annadurai, M. Karunanidhi took over as chief minister in 1969. His leadership of the DMK was challenged by the famous film actor M. G. Ramachandran (MGR) who then left to form his own party, the All India Anna Dravida Munnetra Kazhagam (AIADMK). Typically MGR played heroic roles where as a saviour of the masses he would bring down the rich and rescue the poor and vulnerable. His performances as the common man had a great deal of mass appeal which was a big part of the reason he became such a popular public icon with a large political base.

In the late sixties, MGR was shot by a fellow actor M. R. Radha, with whom he had acted in twenty-five films. The Radha attack made sensational news in Tamil Nadu. The hero survived, albeit with a bullet permanently lodged in his throat (much like in the movies). MGR was chief minister of the state from 1977 to 1987 and, among other social welfare measures, introduced the pioneering Noon Meals Scheme in all government schools in Tamil Nadu (Kamaraj's earlier meal scheme was more limited). For this and other reasons he gained a reputation for philanthropy that heightened the public's veneration of him.

After his death, J. Jayalalithaa, the articulate film actress who is the current chief minister of the state, took over the party leadership, but not without difficulty. She endured a great deal of public humiliation at the hands of her political rivals (including an infamous incident where she was physically assaulted in the Legislature building) before consolidating her position. However enigmatic her persona, there is never any doubt about her acumen. The theatre personality, R. S. Manohar, who was once on a film set with her, has a story about her that he often repeats. Apparently, he found her reading a heavy tome, the pages of which she turned very swiftly. When she was finished with it he teased her, suggesting she had merely skimmed it. 'You can ask me questions,' the young actress said. He asked her a dozen questions and she answered each one correctly, down to identifying the page number that the answer could be found on.

Over the last several decades the people of the state have alternately elected one Dravidian party or the other. The DMK patriarch Karunanidhi has served as chief minister five times. Playwright, scriptwriter and journalist, he has had a long career in politics, first with the Dravida Kazhagam and then with Annadurai, with whom he strengthened the DMK. His bitter enmity with Jayalalithaa is exemplified, among other things, by the plethora of cases that each has filed against the other. They have also made frequent attempts to put each other in jail.

In July 1996, when the DMK government decreed by a gazette notification the name change from Madras to Chennai, there were many who were dismayed, but for others, especially the ruling elite, it was a reassertion of the native identity, much as had happened in other cities of modern India. There was no real organized opposition to the name change, and today while Chennai elbows its way into the landscape of global mega cities, tagging along with it an uneven development yet filled with hope for the future, Madras remains in the ways of life that some of us knew. Ranjitha Ashok, a long-time friend, humour columnist and author of the book *Chennai Latte*, tells me that Madras and Chennai continue to exist in parallel for her. It is not just about colonial nostalgia, she tells me, but about a past that belongs to a certain generation; 'about what one would call the Madras personality that is unapologetic about its Madrasness'. This will of course fade in terms of live memory. But I have no doubt that the two names with which the city started (Madrasapatnam which gave way to Madras and Chennapatnam which birthed Chennai) will continue to have an influence on aspects of the city well into its future. And history keepers will tell and retell this city's stories as both Madras and Chennai in the pages of books, in its music, its art and culture; and some of us will also always remember.

THE LAYERED CITY

The French philosopher and Jesuit scholar, Michel de Certeau, in a brilliant chapter called 'Walking in the City' in his book *The Practice of Everyday Life* points out that the city as planned and run by governments, managers and urban planners is distinct from the city of those who walk in it. Like the flaneur in Paris, the walker in a large city has a different experience than the planner, observes de Certeau. 'Their story begins on ground level, with footsteps. They are myriad, but do not compose a series. They cannot be counted... They weave places together. In that respect pedestrian movements form one of these "real systems whose existence in fact makes up the city". They are not localized; it is rather they that spatialize.' In a memorable exposition that has impacted modern cultural studies, Certeau's insight contrasts the values of those who live in it with the imagined and planned world of those who plan and run the city. The city of Chennai too lies beyond the work of those who imagined it and created it. As I pace the streets, pause and re-examine familiar spaces and landscapes and sometimes drive slowly through its wide roads trying to locate that which is special and singular, I can see that interlinked with the physical space and its history are the stories remembered and half-forgotten, sometimes distorted and reinvented, of people, of families and communities whose lives have made the city. As I look for perspectives and insights from others whose experience of the city is as distinct as mine, I realize how impossible it is to compose a linear and totalizing view of a living breathing, organic whole that the city is.

Walking (not an easy thing in this city) and driving through Chennai's streets now with the intent to relearn, to realign memory and fact, is like recasting the city in a new light—childhood memories, adult interactions and knowledge, much of it a careless acquisition, is now re-examined; in that sense I gain a new awareness of my home ground. As a child, on what seemed like a long drive down the Marina in the back of my parents' car hearing the hum of their conversation, I recall shaking off my somnolence to look curiously at the landscape outside whenever we crossed Napier's Bridge, which was also known as Iron Bridge. For some reason, we would always turn back after going round the War Memorial, which was just beyond Iron Bridge, and drive back towards home. It seemed to me that Iron Bridge was the everyday border of my city although I knew that the 'town' where we went for special purchases was beyond that. To the right was Madras Port, and behind the huge forbidding gates I imagined the tall ships docked, coming in from other shores. And when I learned Masefield's poem, whenever I went by that road, the words always came: 'Quinquireme of Nineveh from distant Ophir/Rowing home to haven', although there were no tall ships, and all that was visible on the bay beyond were the chugging coasters like the dirty British ones in the poem. Only later did I realize that a few hundred yards down that same road was the Fort where it all began.

As I have said at the outset this is a tale of two cities—Madras and Chennai—and these in turn, frame several mini cities; perhaps 'ooru', meaning 'town' or 'place', is a better way of describing these mini cities.

Madras to me is my childhood, ringed by the light of fading summer evenings, cloudless blue skies and a small whisper of a breeze that would offer relief after humid afternoons. Madras is Munro's statue, long drives in my father's Plymouth down the Marina and all the way across Iron Bridge. It meant Jafar's ice cream, cool red cement floors in old houses with high ceilings. It meant the sweet smell of earth stirred by an unexpected shower on a blistering hot May day, and the softness of my mother's Mysore silk sari with the gold brocade mangoes, and a sense that all was well with the world.

Chennai is the world of my adulthood, and the change from a more familiar landscape to one dotted with growing signs of prosperity, a global city on the one hand and a deepening squalor tucked away amid dark side streets on the other. It is a city where it is possible for a girl from a fishing community, a first generation learner, to quickly gain a fortune through a television game show and thereby transform her family's economic status. It is a city which is seeking an international identity through its IT parks, its Kentucky Fried Chicken outlets and its Pizza Huts. Yet it is a city that cannot forego its coffee and idlis and its potti kadais (small shops). There are many cities and oorus within Chennai, as there were many cities within Madras, and as I explored this landscape of home, I realized that the neighbourhoods, the streets and walls, the buildings and alleyways each had a tale to tell of lives ordinary and extraordinary, lived and forgotten, of memories made and of dreams and aspirations that continually added layers and texture to a living history.

The physical world of Madras that became Chennai is therefore also about its small streets and ordinary dwellings—it is about simple and often gullible folk who move to the city from rural hinterlands in search of a better life, but instead fall prey to petty crime, pickpockets and tricksters. This kind of Dickensian view of the city, while represented by a few writers, is largely missing from many mainstream chronicles. There are however works in Tamil that depict the lives and struggles of ordinary citizens from colonial times to the present. A. R. Venkatachalapathy, in a fascinating essay titled 'Street Smart in Chennai' in his book *In Those Days There Was No Coffee*, draws from works like Doosi Rajagopala Boopathy's *Mathimosa Vilakkam* and depicts the early criminal network in the city, and writes of its underbelly.

Whether it is the story of streets like these or old

George Town, where merchants and foreign traders like the Jews and Armenians brought with them the cultures of distant lands and distinct ways of living, or the even more ancient Tiruvallikeni or Triplicane, haunted by the lyrics of poet saints and much later by Bharathi's songs of freedom, the city's multi-tier history is alive and visible. Each locality is suffused with its own colour, its record of settlement and growth over decades and centuries, each has been sheared by time's changes but its individuality still stands. Each locality is defined and often unique but it blends and contributes to the larger tapestry of the city that is Chennai today.

ENGA OORU—'OUR TOWN'

Dr A. Srivathsan, architect, author, specialist in urban planning and a senior editor at *The Hindu*, points out that the territorial imagination of different communities and people within a city's framework is interesting. They all use the word ooru when they refer to adjacent areas. So this kind of imagining of the city is very different, and even if one knows that this is now one large city, the old language prevails. The kuppam or cluster of huts is seen as a distinct ooru. 'There is a distinct spatial imagination which is anthropologically anchored,' Srivathsan tells me. It seemed to me that this was particularly relevant in the case of Madras, especially as I mentioned earlier, as it is, after all, an agglomeration of several villages. In my conversations with Gnanasekaran, a fisherman with whom I spent some time in connection with this book, I recall his poignant notion of the city not extending beyond beach road, the road bordering the Marina. While we stood by the fishing boats, he turned to the road which indeed looked distant at that point even to me and said, 'My feeling of ooru doesn't really extend beyond that bus stand on the road. What is Chennai city to me?'

The notion of one's immediate environment as being nearly all of the world, albeit in the context of Gnanasekaran's perspective, is an indication of social exclusion and underscores the idea of many cities within the city. 'The sense of ooru is also a way of getting into collective memory,' says Srivathsan.

But let us go back even before the Madras/Chennai story began. A string of ancient scattered villages on the Coromandel Coast, some of them threaded together like random stones on a necklace, grew from their small and sometimes sacred beginnings into centres of trade, commerce, pilgrimage and prosperity. Further in were other oorus, equally old, which were all ultimately drawn into the fold of the created city of Madras. Among these, Mayilapur (now Mylapore), Tiruvallikeni (Triplicane), San Thome (Santhome), Tiruvottiyur and, further south, Thiruvanmiyur and Thiruvidanthai, were near the coastline. Villages like Egmore, (its original name was Ezhumbur before it was anglicized to Egmore), Poonamallee, Padi, Manali, Madambakkam and Adambakkam were further inland and are all very much a part of Chennai today.

'Many of these villages, including the interior ones

with their ancient temples, which are a part of today's Chennai, easily date back to the Chola and Pallava times,' says Dr Chithra Madhavan, whose personal connect to the city (apart from the fact that her family belongs to Chennai) is that of a historian specializing in temple architecture, sculpture and medieval inscriptions. Chithra is passionate about the preservation of Chennai's ancient heritage. However, she wears her expertise lightly and patiently explains how the city which we now call home was a region replete with a layered history dating back to villages and settlements that were probably first established as early as the third or fourth century CE, when the Pallavas held sway in south India, and later, after their decline, the great Chola kings of the Tamils were in control of the vast region that included present-day Chennai.

A locality like Santhome, now an extension of Mylapore, whose origin is steeped in the legend of St Thomas (after whom the small seaside village was named) and was later developed into a town by the Portuguese, still reveals facets of this heritage in many of its buildings, its houses and street names. Even today as one criss-crosses its streets, it is very apparent that this was once a separate town, the 'ooru' with a flourishing population that still gives the area a distinct personality.

The Portuguese, who came to the area to trade in the early sixteenth century, actually built the town of San Thome at the edge of the older village of Mylapore and named it after the saint. By 1582 it was a large settlement, and it was fortified against attack by the building of a city wall. Soon there was a large population of Portuguese within this wall. But they could not stay long; British ascendancy in neighbouring Fort St George was a constant threat. The town itself was taken twice by the Sultan of Golconda and once by the French, then came into the custody of one of the Nawabs of the Carnatic from whom the British cunningly wrested it.

The Santhome of today keeps its distinct personality although its borders are blurred. Its streets flow into Mylapore at its western end while the east and the north merge into Marina Beach road. The south leads to Adyar and to Greenways Road and beyond. But in the lime-washed walls of old garden houses (houses surrounded by extensive gardens with flowering shrubs and trees), in the cul-de-sacs and smaller streets with names like Sullivan Street and Nimmo Street, it is possible to glimpse the tracks of another time. A few of the garden houses are still in private hands, but many have been brought down or altered while a few others function as offices of the Church or as educational institutions. Brodie Castle, an imposing colonial building, still retains much of its eighteenth-century structure although it is now government property and houses the Tamil Nadu College of Music. At the other end of Santhome is Leith Castle, another grand, privately owned garden house retaining much of its colonial charm. This building actually came up on the site of the historic Santhome Redoubt built by the British. Like many of Chennai's colonial houses, Leith Castle is half-hidden by shady gardens and shrubs, and with its large verandahs, colonnades, arches and shuttered windows is typical of many of the houses that were a special feature of old Madras. The penchant for creating gardens in Santhome was not limited to private residences. The several churches in the locality are marked by spacious compounds and lovely gardens even to this day.

Another of the 'old towns' of Madras which was first a village is Ezhumbur, known today as Egmore, an area at the heart of modern Chennai. The antiquity of the settlement has been established as it is described in two inscriptions in the northern wall of the Parthasarathy Temple in Triplicane. The date of the inscription is 1309; the inscription mentions that 'Ezhumur nadu' was an administrative unit during Chola rule (obviously there was a highly evolved structure of governance). Dr R. Nagaswamy, the former Director of the Tamil Nadu Department of Archaeology, points out to me that the use of the term 'nadu' (loosely meaning 'country') along with 'Ezhumur' probably indicates that this was one of the larger administrative units. He adds that it had agricultural activity and many residential settlements around it, and that this probably remained intact until the end of the fifteenth century.

In the course of the East India Company's expansion fanning out from Fort St George, the village of Ezhumbur was acquired in 1693 and became the site of a military outpost. In time the name mutated to Egmore. This continued as a distinct locality for quite some time, having been a separate 'ooru' once. It's still easy to see this as the area bends within the curve of the Cooum (navigable during colonial times but now mostly dry in places or filled with dank, polluted water) and because of the ample green all around, some of which is thankfully still in place, it stands out as one of the more airy and expansive parts of the city. The large residences with big compounds that first came up soon became home to wealthy British merchants and officers, followed by wealthy Indians. Muthiah writes that to the west of Egmore when the more wealthy among the Chettiars began to buy houses and settle there, that particular area came to be known as Chetti Pettai, now known as Chetpet. He also points out that the great builder of the nineteenth century, Madras T. Namberumal Chetty, owned 2,000 grounds and 99 houses in this area. The story goes that he did not want to get the hundredth one for astrological reasons! Namberumal Chetty constructed the Victoria Memorial Hall, the Government Museum, the Victoria Technical Institute, the Connemara Library and the Madras Law College among others. He himself lived in a beautiful colonial mansion called Crynant which he bought from a British officer in 1858. The mathematical genius Srinivasa Ramanujan was regarded by Chetty as his own son and spent his last few years in one of his grand residences. (Namberumal Chetty was also the first Indian to own a car in Madras.)

Some of the most important public buildings in the city are located in Egmore. Historic Pantheon Road was so named because of The Pantheon, the name given to public assembly rooms where a lot of Greek plays were staged. This fell into disrepair after 1830, although parts of the building are still visible behind the Connemara Library. Then there is the beautiful Museum Theatre in the Government Museum grounds, built in semi-circular style, still the scene of many performances (thanks to the recent air conditioning) in the city. The long-standing Madras Players, the best-known and much loved amateur English theatre group, has given Chennai audiences some memorable theatre experiences in these premises.

The Government Museum, known as the Madras Museum and established in 1851, is the second oldest museum in the country after Kolkata's. The famed bronze gallery in this museum is known to have made visitors weep at the sheer beauty of some of the exhibits. However, there has been a stream of continuous criticism from visitors and experts alike about the way in which much of the display is set up and exhibited.

The National Art Gallery, another beautiful building in red sandstone, is also in the Museum complex. Much of the environment and facilities both inside and outside however could do with repairs and better upkeep.

Egmore is also home to schools and hospitals and the Madras Literary Society Library, which originally functioned within the Museum complex and was connected to the Connemara Library until it moved to nearby premises. Muthiah recounts a lovely story of how the library idea first took off in Madras in 1662, when a bale of calico from the city was sent all the way to London in exchange for books, after which a second consignment was sent for and maintained in a standing library at Fort House in Fort St George.

PRESERVING THE TIERS OF HISTORY

The politics of heritage and conservation has been an issue in Chennai. In recent decades, the Indian National Trust for Art and Cultural Heritage (INTACH) chapter in Chennai, which is a non-governmental organization working to preserve and conserve heritage structures has, along with other private groups, supported conservation initiatives in the city. Like the buildings in Egmore, there are numerous buildings in Chennai in the Indo-Saracenic style. Many of these buildings and their precincts date back over two hundred to three hundred years. In the absence of specific heritage laws (long on the anvil but not created), every case where historic buildings needed protection has relied on the court's intervention to protect the edifices.

The Bharat Insurance building on Anna Salai is a case in point. Even though it has been long neglected, the beautiful red brick structure has always caught the eye of the discerning passer-by with its gracefully designed balconies, tall minarets and stained glass windows that refract the light into a million pieces. When the Life Insurance Corporation bought the building some years ago and tried to demolish it, INTACH filed a public interest litigation for its preservation. When the High Court ruled against the demolition, the owners moved the Supreme Court, which stayed the matter and referred it to the Heritage Commission. In another instance, during the earlier administration of the present chief minister, the government sought to demolish the Queen Mary's College building, and also tried to pull down the police headquarters on the Marina (both colonial buildings); there was a great deal of public protest that prevented these demolitions. While the surprising spontaneity of public reaction was heartening, there is no uniform application of any principle of restoration and maintenance that prevails. P. T. Krishnan, one of Chennai's leading architects, who has also served as the convener of INTACH, and is on the National Commission of Heritage and Restoration, in a recent conversation expressed a great deal of disappointment and anguish about the present state of affairs. He stressed in particular the lack of a proper policy and approach to restoration and conservation in the city.

Another aspect that makes restoration and conservation a challenge in the city is an inadequate awareness of the great cultural heritage of the region, Chithra Madhavan tells me. Many small temples and ancient structures in different parts of the city have been thoughtlessly modernized with every vestige of antiquity removed. For instance, Chithra says the Karneeshwarar Temple on Bazaar Road, Mylapore, and the Virupaksheshwarar Temple opposite, both had many Chola inscriptions dateable to the ninth century, from scripts and epigraphs which were already fragmentary; traces however remained. 'During successive kumbabishekams, [dedication, or the periodic rededication of temples] polished granite tiles, often more like bathroom tiles were stuck on the walls totally obliterating the original inscriptions. If you pry off the polished granite slabs, the inscriptions come out with it. This is what we have done to our heritage and it is totally tragic,' she says. 'In many cases the sculptures and epigraphs are also obliterated by painting over them with chemical paints. There seems to be more and more money available to do all this but less sensitivity,' remarks Chithra ruefully.

It is a matter of some dismay, not just in Chennai, but in many parts of Tamil Nadu, that when ancient temple gopurams and pillars are renovated, they are painted in bright colours, with a sense of abandon that bounces off the registers of aestheticism. As Chithra tells me, 'It is a lack of awareness that a temple, even one that is very damaged and crumbling, can be restored with much of the original material. Much of it can be rebuilt as there are trained conservationists who can do this, but they are rarely consulted.'

'And what about the Archaeological Survey of India?' I ask. The ASI has about 450 monuments under its care in Tamil Nadu, Chithra tells me, and all of them are well maintained, but others are under the state government or run by private trusts and the ASI cannot step into these. However, there is apparently some cause for cheer. She tells me of a small but ancient Chola temple in Madambakkam, in the suburbs of

Chennai close to Tambaram, which was in an utter state of decay, when the ASI stepped in. The result is a perfectly intact Chola temple, with Vijayanagara inscriptions and sculptures from a later era. 'This is just one hamlet in today's Chennai,' says Chithra, adding, 'and there are very many such hamlets everywhere in greater Chennai.' She mentions a place called Manimangalam, another old village with an ancient Rajagopalaswamy Temple where the traditional Vaishnavite symbols—the sanka and chakra—are mysteriously reversed. Chitra tells me that the place is actually the site of a fierce battle fought between the Chola ruler's armies and those of the invading Chalukyas. Another ancient hamlet is Oonamanjeri close to the Vandalur Zoo. 'I always joke that when I turn off the twenty-first-century highway on the Kelambakkam Road and wend my way through potholed roads to Oonamanjeri, I go back in time to the sixteenth century, for at the end of that dirt track is an exquisite Vijayanagara temple,' she laughs.

THE LAYERS OF DEPRIVATION

A different kind of demolition also gets ruthlessly executed in the city; and it is not about buildings but people. The poor and the powerless get shifted out of their environment, where they have eked out a living for generations, giving their all to keep the city running. I met a group of dislocated people one morning in Kannagi Nagar, a government-created low-income township wedged between the spanking new IT corridor called 'Old' Mahabalipuram Road, and the 'new' Mahabalipuram Road that runs parallel to the sea. Here, families of four or six people are housed in matchbox structures, whose total dimensions measure roughly ten feet by twelve feet, next to open sewers infested with flies and mosquitoes.

Aloysius Xavier Lopez, a singular young journalist (whose commitment to social vulnerability and deprivation issues leaves me filled with hope for a more socially just Chennai in the future) accompanies me to the Kannagi Nagar resettlement. Many of the people here are fishermen who have been forcibly relocated from areas near the sea, and promised rehabilitation, new dwellings with good infrastructure, good schools and virtually a new lease of life. Their original dwellings were battered by the tsunami of December 2006 that devastated much of Chennai's coastline. A sizable number had also been 'resettled' by the Chennai Slum Clearance Board a few years earlier. Aloysius tells me that many of the promises made at the time they were being relocated were, of course, never kept.

The women I speak to in Kannagi Nagar are especially angry. 'We were promised much by the government,' says Rani, whose husband was murdered by members of a criminal gang in her presence. 'Whether it is the government or the police, none of them care about us,' she says. 'We work for this city but we get nothing in return. As women, we have no safety in these slums. And it is especially hard for single women like me. I live in constant fear of violence. Assaults on women are common both within households and on the streets,' she says angrily.

I also meet Renuka and Radha, two young girls who invite me to their houses. An open gutter runs just outside the ramshackle apartment block where both live with their families. The smell of uncleared garbage rises in the air. 'We are beauticians,' they say in unison. 'Where do you work?' I ask. 'In a nearby beauty parlour,' says Renuka, who is probably around twenty years old. 'I am not qualified formally. I had to work after school to support my widowed mother and brothers and sisters. I learned the trade from another beauty parlour close by where they employed me as a cleaner, but I wanted to do something better with my life than be just a maid or a cleaner.' Her eyes are full of hope. Radha, who is probably around the same age, says she acquired a diploma at a small beauty institute to get her present job. 'I want to open my own beauty parlour one day,' she says, 'but my parents want me to get married soon and then I don't know what will happen.' She seems resigned to her fate. As I continue speaking to them I realize that what they both really want besides economic self-sufficiency is to escape from the squalor of their surroundings. The city is a harsh theatre for the staging of their lives.

MAMIS ON SCOOTERS

But a quick shift of scene in the city takes you into another kind of world, a world where old Madras and new Chennai meet, an upper-crust Chennai which, however, unlike other high-end city spots, strangely does not exude typical snobbery. Currently, it is considered the city's 'happening' place much in the way that some clubs were in earlier times.

This is Amethyst Cafe, probably one of South Chennai's most popular age-immune gathering places, catering to a diverse clientele ranging from not-so-furtive young lovers to giggling groups of college girls. Many of Chennai's lunching ladies, who often seem as much weighed down by their designer handbags as their secretly burdensome lives, are also visible. Considering the number of foreigners and young people who gather here, all exhibiting a kind of global sartorial uniformity, this could be anywhere in the world. There is a flower shop to the right of the cafe patronized by the city's elite, with exotic offerings flown in from cities like Bangalore, and arrangements that are quite ingenious and take one's breath away. Up a gorgeous old wooden staircase is a vast expanse of space laid out under an industrial style steel roof with museum-like focus lighting. Here the discerning open their purses for designer wear and distinctive jewellery that is not available in most other shops in the city. The brainchild of Kiran Rao, Amethyst was originally located in an old family bungalow where it quickly became one of the city's favourite eating and meeting spots. When Kiran had to move to Whites Road, a more corporate location amidst the rush and bustle of busy, where garages and automobile showrooms dominate the landscape, she managed to create a verdant forest of tall palms and green foliage that bordered an open wrap-around verandah. Inside the tearoom, furnished in a delightful mixture of whimsical and classical, are posters that are a comic take on traditional themes; and comfortable sofas where people linger over eclectic fare at lunch and teatime. The slow, old grace of a city blends with the spirit of the times.

Kiran tells me that she left Chennai when she was fifteen. When she came back she felt that all that was charming had disappeared and that Chennai had deteriorated. 'For instance, sitting and having a conversation on a verandah was a peculiarly Madras thing,' she says. 'I felt you needed places like that in view of the changing dynamics of the city. We were the first to do this in Chennai. When I first came back to Chennai everything was either five-star or shabby. And I thought, why shouldn't there be an in-between space which doesn't have air conditioning maybe, but can still offer a high level of service and many other things that create a great ambience and environment.' Kiran points to the lush green foliage around her. She adds, 'I think that traditional Chennai comes here because it has resonance for them. The posh bankers come because for them it's an inverted sense of chic. There's always been an understated chic in Madras. I also get young kids who don't have similar hangout places in the city. Chennai is less reticent and insular than it used to be. I also think one of the reasons why I came back is that I'm a small town girl and Chennai is in some ways essentially a small town.'

Sitting late one afternoon on Amethyst's wide verandah, I look at the three remarkable women around me, three friends from childhood, and if I half close my eyes, I can see the little girls they were when I first knew them. We all drink peppermint tea in a subconscious emphasis of our links with one another and I listen to what they have to say about the city they grew up in. And as I look at them through the lens of old and affectionate friendship, I can see that Chennai is the same city it has been to them; two of them are not Tamil but have grown up here and although all three of them left their childhood spaces and lived away as young adults, they each came back at various points in their lives to a changed Chennai.

'Chennai has changed though tradition still remains,' says management consultant Bablu Thomas, 'but the city has adapted well to change. All those old mamis are very much around and you can drink your filter coffee and wear Kanchipuram saris, but what is amazing is that they are all so comfortable with technology.'

Vidya Singh, who runs an events company and is an erstwhile princess of Vijayanagara adds, 'You have mamis rushing about on scooters wearing a madisar (the near defunct nine-yard sari worn by orthodox Brahmin women) and a helmet. There is in fact an elderly lady who is called "scooter mami", who zips about on her scooter doing various cooking jobs in houses. There is a false notion that the city is very traditional; actually Chennai is full of progressive citizens. Just because you wear a silk sari, it doesn't mean that you are conservative.'

The writer Ranjitha Ashok had expressed a similar sentiment during one of our conversations earlier. 'The conservative label is worn with élan in Chennai,' she said. 'It is a likeable Chennai trait; the same Tamil woman who will do her pujas regularly every morning will also be seen twirling a mojito at a cocktail party in the evening. The same woman may wear designer shoes in today's Chennai, but will be careful not to step on a kolam with it,' Ranjitha pointed out.

Rita Chaudhuri, who has many years of experience in corporate management and currently coaches CEOs and executives, observes that the people of Chennai seem to have a special ability to adapt, survive and manage between diverse worlds. She feels that the city nourishes specific skills and services in the medical field, in automobiles, in information technology, in engineering, and in the manufacturing sectors, all of which have boomed in Chennai in recent decades. And the women agree that while there is not much of an entrepreneurial spirit in the city (because of the streak of conservatism that makes the average Chennaite risk-averse) people do know how to nourish and build on old businesses. For example, original British-owned companies like Simpson and Co. were handed over to enterprising Indian employees, who have taken these companies forward. There is no flamboyance about these old businesses, the women remark, and the notion of noblesse oblige is strong, so they take care of not just their employees but extend their paternalistic largesse to many of their favourite causes.

The appreciation of the intrinsic worth of people as opposed to their physical wealth is considered a dominant Chennai attribute. Along with this are values of tolerance and inclusiveness, coupled with simplicity of lifestyle. My friends call this the 'bush shirt and white veshti' lifestyle, one that symbolizes the understated externality covering an enormous (and usually inherited) family fortune. These are probably the city's core values, albeit limited to one elite strand of its citizenry, muse the ladies. There is also an innate sense of generosity and its citizens seem to have a distinct sporting spirit. Vidya recalls a famous India-Pakistan cricket match where the winning Pakistani team got a standing ovation from the masses that thronged the stadium. This is what Chennai is all about, the ladies say. 'In Bombay, when Pakistan won a match, the cricket pitch was dug up by goons,' says Vidya. 'And Chennai was also the only place where not a stone was thrown when the Babri Masjid was brought down. There were no riots in this city but only peaceful protest marches,' Vidya recollects.

Yet Bablu reminds us that when the core of Chennai or Madras is touched, there is always a strong reaction. During the anti-Hindi riots in 1965 against the imposition of Hindi for example, there was violence and arson that lasted well over two months. As very young children, these women only remember the fears of the adults around them and the restrictions imposed on their movements; but the memory stands out, because unlike other cities Chennai tends to be largely peaceable.

I myself recall another situation when MGR, the hugely popular chief minister, died. We were on the road in three cars heading to the airport with the children in the back seats, ready to fly out to Bangalore. When an emotional crowd surrounded us threateningly, telling us to stop and join in their grief, we fearfully did what they asked us to. Although the cars were not allowed to ply the roads and had to be abandoned, the menacing crowd suddenly melted away with murmurs of 'There are children', and 'Let's leave them alone'. Whether or not those people were moved by the old man's passing, they were at least moved enough by our vulnerable situation to let us go. Like many other urban agglomerations, especially where there are huge disparities in incomes and lifestyles, the sense of menace lies just below the surface in Chennai and when the elements of a situation align in a certain way, matters could certainly get out of hand.

As my friends delve deeper into aspects of the city, other not-so-comfortable characteristics of their beloved Madras emerge. Rita remarks how an American friend married to an Indian, who had lived in Chennai for several years, felt that she could never penetrate the heart of the city. Chennai is a city of secret societies, her friend had commented, and the women acknowledge that the insider circles of the city close within themselves, making it hard for outsiders to enter. The city's clubs are usually the snobbish fulcrum from which some of these circles emerge. There is a business owners' group, for instance, who imagine that they are deciding the fate of the nation over beers at posh clubs each evening; then there are some expats who keep to themselves, fearful perhaps of the propensities of Indian culture. Senior civil servants who gain entry into some of these clubs form a tight-knit group as they cynically confer on the problems of governance in the state and country. Then there are clusters of women who get together over regular lunches at the city's top-end eating places, trading gossip, fashion tips and the newest diet secrets. These diverse circles are mostly inviolate and tightly-knit except perhaps for the occasional infiltration.

Outside the quiet fascism of some of these groupings are other, perhaps more democratic, circles which allow for easier entry—examples being college groups, mami groups, coffee klatches and bhajan (religious singing) groups. Interestingly, in recent years, small book clubs, art clubs and music appreciation groups have also sprung up in various parts of the city.

There is also another layer of men and women who are quite outside the pale of these social formations and who work incessantly to keep the engines of the city running. They have little time for leisure except perhaps during the occasional holiday or festival when they may go off in small groups and tour temples or visit ancestral places around the region.

THE FAULT LINES OF PREJUDICE

While there is no actual ghettoization in terms of communities, there are areas in the city where larger numbers of specific ethnic and minority groups tend to settle. For instance, north of George Town in Sowcarpet there are many Marwari families who originally came to Madras over a century ago. In Triplicane, near the mosque, there are large settlements of Muslims and in Vepery there are a number of Anglo-Indian families. The fault lines are subtle, unlike perhaps in other cities. In lifestyle matters there are some telltale signs of prejudice. A Muslim cook would find it easier to find work in a Christian household than a Hindu one, say my friends. When apartments are rented out in some pockets of the city there are sometimes specific qualifiers like 'vegetarians only', which is of course a euphemism for caste preferences.

While the city rightfully prides itself on its largely secular credentials, sometimes bigotry and discrimination raise their menacing heads. It is true that caste clashes are more common in Chennai than outbreaks of communal violence but in recent years a subtle shift seems to have occurred, mirroring the national landscape, where biases and prejudices against a minority population often come into play.

I had several lengthy conversations with S. Anvar, the documentary filmmaker and photographer currently researching Tamil Muslims. I was struck by his journey from a purely Tamil identity to one that has expanded to include a strong awareness of his cultural and religious heritage that hasn't compromised on a wider vision 'of tolerance and sharing', as he puts it. Growing up in a family that was politically aware (close family members were connected to the DMK), as a child he only knew about the anti-Hindi mood that was then prevalent in the state. He really did not connect with the local Islamic clergy although he says, 'The demolition of the Babri Masjid did trouble me, but then Ayodhya was a distant place and I was too young to understand its implications.' It was only later in 1995, when he was assisting Avinash Pasricha, a Delhi-based photographer, that he was first confronted with prejudice. They were photographing Ripon Building (where the Chennai Corporation has its offices) when they saw 'a few officials shouting security objections and running towards us. I took it upon myself to talk to them but they were not satisfied', says Anvar. When he gave them his business card, one official 'took one look at it, then shook his head saying, "Your name is Anvar. This is definitely a problem." I was taken aback and tried to laugh it off. "Don't laugh, with a name like that it could mean real trouble," he warned me. I lost my cool and told him that I would complain about him…I couldn't believe that someone would consider me a risk because of my name and faith.'

This disturbing incident and later the fallout from the riots in Coimbatore, where families of Muslims who were killed were not adequately compensated by the government, shook him deeply. 'It took me two years to emerge from the "minority mentality",' he says.

In his research on Tamil Muslims and the history of Islam in the city, Anvar says he was greatly helped by

Muthiah, who mentored him. He recalls other situations where even so-called experts in South Indian heritage and history revealed an astonishing level of prejudice and ignorance. One person told him, 'You Muslims do everything in reverse.' And this from a man who gave lectures on South India! Anvar explained to him saying if his argument was based on the way Arabic is written and read, Arabic is not Islam. He pointed out that Arabic is not a divine language for Muslims, but just a language that is written differently like Chinese. But the man was not convinced. There were other instances and encounters that Anvar told me about, such as Muslims being referred to as 'thulukkan', which is a derogatory way of addressing them. This is another layer that the city often masks where, when the veneer of education comes off, crude prejudice is in evidence. Worse still, there is sometimes an unwillingness to move beyond illogical biases and ignorance even in a city that prides itself on its secular credentials.

Listening to Anvar, I am amazed by the depth of his knowledge, not just on the rich history of Muslims and the journey of Islam in south India, but on his penetrating insights into the history and culture of India as a whole (he had earlier made a film on the Brihadeeswara Temple in Thanjavur which was commissioned by the ASI). He quotes something that Shashi Tharoor once said, '...we are all minorities in India.' Anvar tells me, 'You are either a religious or a caste or a linguistic minority. A South Indian is a minority in Shiv Sena's Mumbai, a Sikh is a minority in

Delhi and so on. In a nation of minorities, I guess we are all equals. It depends on how you see the glass, half-filled or half empty. I see it half-filled.' The richness of thought and feeling I heard from him, clothed in a language of gentle civility over several hours and days of conversation, often left me profoundly moved.

NEW MONEY AND THE GLOBAL OORU

New money, largely from politically connected families as well as software and BPO services have created a nouveau riche, whose large houses and expensive cars fuel a new kind of race towards acquisitions and material gains.

Some of the new software money emanates from Chennai's software corridor, also known as Old Mahabalipuram Road or OMR. Once a narrow, sleepy road with coconut groves and rice fields on either side, it is now a frenetic, multi-lane arterial road. The groves and fields have been replaced by gleaming glass-and-chrome buildings, housing thousands of information technology professionals serving the rest of the world and boosting the economy of the home state. Large companies like Cognizant Technologies, Tata Consultancy Services (TCS), Wipro and Infosys have their global back-office services based here. This is the new location for technological growth and proudly works to reinforce Chennai as a twenty-first-century global city.

OMR stretches far from the core of Chennai, and

consequently large, modern apartment buildings, schools, hospitals, hotels, colleges and shopping complexes have sprung up on or near the busy thoroughfare for the convenience of those who work in its environs. Drive along OMR at any time of the day or night and you will bear witness to incessant traffic, bustling commerce and the feeling that resting or sleeping here is definitely against the law.

Curiously, the many gated residential communities that have sprung up around these neighbourhoods seek to replicate the symbols of the older Madras culture. My friend Radha Hegde, who is a professor of media, culture and communication at New York University and is from Chennai, speaks of how interesting it is that along with trying to sell apartments in these new developments, they speak of providing an ambience and features that will be just like their original homes ('We bring Mylapore to OMR' says one slogan).

In addition, other hallmarks of globalization such as shopping malls and luxury stores selling high-end brands have come to stay in Chennai. Although Chennai's well-heeled may be perceived as careful spenders, retailers feel that this attitude is changing, and whether it be a Louis Vuitton handbag or a Jaguar XK, Chennai is ready to buy and ready to pay. One must note however that the reverse also holds true. Many quintessentially Chennai brands, like Nalli (silk saris), Saravana Bhavan (restaurant) now have an international presence. As Chennai imports the hallmarks of a global ooru, there is also a reverse globalization in play, and bits of Chennai can be found in cities around the world.

As I walk the streets meeting people and talking to them about their lives and their notions of the city as well as their hopes and dreams for the future, I realize that the cities within cities may be separate but are bridged by mutual dependence, and perhaps even a sense of community. These people may have diverse aspirations and interests and belong to different social groups; yet they are all united by a common dream—that the city will fulfil their hopes and dreams, give their children and their children's children a good life. It is what unites the highest to the lowest, the computer programmer to the slum dweller, and while it might well be a dream without foundation in the case of the majority of the city's inhabitants, it is the glue that holds the city's many layers together.

OF PERFORMANCE AND SPECTACLE

There is a breathlessness about Chennai in December.
It begins calmly enough in the mornings when the soft strains of *Tiruppavai*, the devotional hymn composed by Andal, the seventh-century woman saint, are heard in prayerful but melodic strains across the city. In T. Nagar and Thiruvanmiyur, in Triplicane and Mylapore, in many houses and in temples, the thirty verses of Andal are regularly chanted. The hymn depicts elements of personal faith and service to the Supreme Being or Narayana through the poetry of surrender, the quintessence of the philosophy of Vaishnavism. In celebration of the general atmosphere of piousness that is on display this month, many homes are thoroughly cleaned, and their entrances are decorated with kolams. Temples distribute delicious prasadam to worshippers. As the day progresses into early evening and night, the city bustles with movement as the world's largest classical music show gets going.

In no other city can you witness more than a hundred concerts or performances a day, adding up to perhaps two thousand during the month. These take place in smart concert halls as well as on makeshift stages located in schools and wedding halls (all called sabhas), all located within a few yards of each other. Old men shivering in mufflers and monkey caps, worn as protection against the mildly cool temperatures of December evenings that seldom fall below 20 degrees Celsius, elderly mamis decked out in diamonds and silk saris are crowded into the same space as the young in their deliberately casual jeans but crisp shirts (a nod to the formality of the ambience). Some come from within the city, some from the suburbs. Many non-resident Indians on their annual visits home come eager to savour and connect with the traditions of music and dance that are unique to Chennai. The greatest musicians and dancers on show are so revered that tickets to their performances command a premium, rather like those of the biggest rock stars in the West.

As the critics and experts descend on the city, lay people, some of whom probably have only an elementary knowledge of Carnatic music, suddenly wax eloquent on the nuances of various ragas and offer authoritative opinions on these subjects. But the music is not the only thing that is sought after. A friend once told me that a middle-aged couple she knew would pretend that they were regular concertgoers when in actual fact what they were doing was savouring the food at the various sabha canteens, hopping from one location to another. The sabhas usually run special catering services throughout the season, and each venue is famous for particular items of food. The caterers are well-established city cooks who run small eateries or cater to large occasions like weddings, but who temporarily set up their services in concert venues. With their grand names like 'Mint' Padmanabhan and 'Mountbatten' Mani Iyer, they run their canteens with all the pomp and precision of a military operation. Many concertgoers enjoy the food at the concert venues as much as the music, so much so, that during the season, most of their meals are had in these places. Some perennial favourites are keera vadai, adai, sambar rice, pineapple rasam and curd rice with fresh pickles. Sometimes, there are even three and four course meals, served the traditional way on fresh banana leaves. In recent times North Indian staples like paneer-based dishes, chaats and samosas have become popular, as Chennai music lovers tend to be an eclectic lot. Of course, the filter coffee at these places, served sweet and piping hot, is another all-time favourite.

During the season, it is classical Carnatic music that predominates among vocalists, and among dance forms, it is Bharatanatyam which is most popular, each dancer interpreting it personally with subtle variations in style and content. Carnatic music came to Chennai from the courts of the Thanjavur kings, from towns like Madurai and Tirunelveli, as the merchants and dubashes who settled in Black Town began to patronize the arts with their growing wealth and influence. The new temples that were built in Black Town, such as the Chenna Kesava Perumal Temple also employed nadaswaram players, odhuvars, and devadasis who moved to the newly established city from towns like Thanjavur and found patrons. It must be mentioned though, that even before the city was established, villages like Tiruvallikeni, Mylapore, Thiruvidanthai, in which ancient temples were located, had a music tradition that sprang from songs sung by Saivite and Vaishnavite saints or mystics as early as the fifth and sixth centuries CE. Their compositions reflected the new cult of personal devotion or bhakti that became popular during the sixth and seventh centuries CE in the region; bhakti worship promoted personal communication with God as opposed to the more formal and distant mode of worship that had been practiced until then. This made religion more accessible to common folk and released it from the stranglehold of caste and organized religion. These hymns were more like musical chants. Because the original musical notations were unknown, many latter-day musicians incorporated into them elements of Carnatic music. These hymns are regularly sung or chanted in Saivite and Vaishnavite temples in the city today.

However, it was only in the seventeenth and eighteenth century, when Thanjavur dominated as the cultural capital of the region with the arts flourishing under the royal patronage of the Marathas (who had by then conquered the area) that Carnatic music made a breakthrough. The contributions of the great musical trinity of Tyagaraja, Muthuswami Dikshithar and Syama Sastri to Carnatic music were tremendous. Tyagaraja is considered the greatest of them all by most practitioners of the art today. Interestingly, according to the writer Indira Menon, who has written an excellent account of women musicians of Chennai in her book *The Madras Quartet*, Tyagaraja who favoured his independence and resisted the royal patronage of Sarabhoji, the Thanjavur ruler, actually incorporated some English band music into a few of his compositions.

Although there were few women musicians performing at this time, devadasis took to the stage as early as the eighteenth century. Devadasis, who performed Bharatanatyam, were ritually dedicated to temples at a very young age and were usually patronized by wealthy men. While in the early years of the city of Madras many of them were accorded some social position as they were usually under the guardianship of one man, neither they nor their children had any rights at all. Indeed, the majority were not only sexually exploited but also forced into prostitution. This brutal exploitation of the devadasis led to a growing Anti-Nautch Movement spearheaded by social reformers like Dr Muthulakshmi Reddy, who was the first woman legislator in British India. She fiercely campaigned against the devadasi system. Although Muthulakshmi met with stiff resistance from several quarters including from political leaders (who felt they needed the status quo to preserve the arts) and even from some dancers themselves, the devadasi system was abolished after a hard-fought battle in 1947.

Dancer Lakshmi Viswanathan in her important book *Women of Pride: The Devadasi Heritage* has elaborately researched and documented the lives of the devadasis and detailed their contributions to the dance legacy of the city today. 'The devadasi's legacy of dance has reinvented itself in a myriad ways', she pointed out, saying that the stature of Bharatanatyam today owes much to their contributions.

Another champion of women's rights was Moovalur Ramamirtham Ammaiyar, initiated into the devadasi system and forced into prostitution by her own parents at a young age. She extended the parameters of the debate even beyond Dr Muthulakshmi Reddy's vision, insisting that the devadasis' voices be heard directly and not just through the representations of reformers. Politically active, first with the Congress party and then with the Self-Respect Movement, she later joined the Dravida Kazhagam, the parent party of the later Dravidian political parties. Although completely self-taught, she wrote a brilliant novel on the devadasis and numerous articles in Tamil magazines which severely criticized the perniciousness of the system.

As their lot began to improve, some of the dancers were emboldened enough to try and break out of the system. One of these was Kamakshi Ammal, who became a student of Syama Sastri. She moved to Madras and found a patron who supported her career. The renowned Veena Dhanammal, whose expertise on the veena overshadowed many male performers of the time, was her granddaughter. The Madras audience would marvel at Dhanam's mellifluous voice, so attuned to her instrument that one could hardly tell which was which, according to those present at her recitals. Indira

Menon says in her book that English officials like Lord Ripon and Lord Carmichael, in addition to local worthies, would attend Dhanammal's concerts. As Dhanammal was extremely proficient in Hindustani music also, the musician Abdul Karim Khan was an admirer, and she welcomed the likes of the singer and dancer Gauhar Jan of Calcutta to her home in Madras. Like Gauhar Jan, Dhanammal allowed her music to be recorded for the gramophone. Her brilliant granddaughters, T. Brinda, T. Mukta and Balasaraswathi inherited her genius, each in her own inimitable style, and with their successes added to their grandmother's legacy. My mother took us to see one of Balasaraswathi's final performances; she was perhaps the greatest dancer of the age. I recall dimly that although we were mildly surprised by her unexceptional appearance, when she moved on to the stage the fluidity, expressiveness and complete grace of her abhinaya mesmerized the audience. My mother, as usual intent on ensuring that her reluctant brood really got it, pointed out the elegance of the aging dancer's movement as she swished an imaginary long plait or performed some other equally subtle abhinaya.

As dance moved out of the temples, experts like E. Krishna Iyer raised its social profile. Rukmini Devi Arundale, whose controversial marriage to Theosophist George Arundale had even *The Hindu* spluttering in outrage, was the person who elevated what was known as sadir (or the solo dance in princely courts) to a level of finesse and social acceptance that soon had all the young girls in Madras clamouring to learn Bharatanatyam. Rukmini Devi established a school for music and the arts called Kalakshetra, with an emphasis on teaching dance. As the dance form became a staple of Chennai culture it threw up a succession of distinguished dancers, among them Padma Subrahmanyam, Chitra Visweswaran, Lakshmi Viswanathan and Sudharani Raghupathy who were an inspiration to those who came after. Later dancers like Malavika Sarukkai, Alarmel Valli, Priyadarsini Govind and Anita Ratnam pushed the boundaries of Bharatanatyam even further, sometimes with choreography, sometimes with their style of performance. Sushila Ravindranath distinctly remembers the flowering of dance in the city. 'I remember Madras discovering Sonal Mansingh, discovering Yamini Krishnamurthy. I remember watching Yamini dance at the Museum Theatre. And suddenly Chennai became the stage for all dance forms, and Kuchipudi became popular.'

In parallel to the rise of dance, was the great flowering of Carnatic music. No account of the music of Madras will be complete without a mention of the great M. S. Subbulakshmi who was the singer par excellence of her time and perhaps of all time. Even as a young child who moved to Madras from Madurai with her musician mother Veena Shanmugavadivu (her father was her mother's patron, but died when Subbulakshmi was a little girl) she showed remarkable talent, and her mesmerizing voice stunned listeners as she came into contact with the great teachers and practitioners of the era. Dhanammal took a keen interest in her, and there were others who taught her the rudiments of classical music. The film *Meera*, in which she was cast by the American director Ellis Dungan (who made many films in India) was a phenomenal success although she soon transitioned to classical Carnatic music, especially after her marriage to Sadasivam, a journalist with two young daughters.

Sadasivam and his friend the great writer, Kalki Krishnamurthy, were close friends with Rajaji and ardent supporters of the freedom struggle. As the fame of MS grew, she was often asked to sing to raise money for the freedom struggle. MS's rendition of *Vaishnava Janatho* and *Hari Tum Haro* moved the Mahatma greatly. Gopalkrishna Gandhi tells me that MS, Sadasivam and Kalki Krishnamurthy were like Rajaji's extended family and he knew her very well. 'She lavished her affection on me and my siblings and while I loved her music, I never really learnt anything about music from her, and neither did she once speak to any of us about it, such was her sweetness and humility. She was basically a favourite aunt,' he recalls. 'I can speak and write about her as a person but not as a musician,' he says. 'It's rather like my knowledge of Madras. I know her as a city but cannot enter her grammar. I find that a bit of a dichotomy,' he smiles.

The music of MS is like one of the languages of the city. In many Chennai households the mornings are marked with her *Suprabhatam* or *Vishnu*

Sahasranamam. Music teachers encourage their students to listen to her recordings as they learn their craft. The memory of her renderings of various krithis or songs has now become part of the city's psyche and she is perhaps the most recognizable voice in the universe of Carnatic music. Indira Menon mentions that the great Yehudi Menuhin was moved to tears by MS's *Bhavayami Gopalabalam* in the raga Yamuna Kalyani.

There were other gifted musicians during that period like D. K. Pattammal and Madras Lalithangi Vasanthakumari or MLV as she was popularly known. V. Sriram showed me the old devadasi quarter in George Town where many of the musicians and dancers who came to the city first settled. He pointed out a house with a green door which looked more like an abandoned warehouse than an establishment that, in its heyday, had been filled with music and the sound of anklets as young dancers trained and young women practiced their music. 'MLV and her mother lived here,' he said. Interestingly, musicians and dancers who came to the city from the Thanjavur courts inherited their art through matrilineal family traditions.

The Music Academy, the city's premier music association, was established in 1928, after the Indian National Congress adopted a resolution to promote Indian classical music. However, there were sabhas such as the Muthialpet Sabha and the Tondaimandalam Sabha that existed before the Academy. (The Muthialpet Sabha awarded a prize for the best original composition in praise of the newly ascended King-Emperor George V to a musician called Ramanathapuram Srinivasa Iyengar.) In 1911, the Sri Parthasarathy Swami Sabha was established in Triplicane, and is the city's oldest surviving sabha today. The Tamil Isai Sangam was set up in 1943 by votaries of Tamil and was supported by wealthy patrons like Annamalai Chettiar. The Sangam's establishment followed a round of conferences where serious debate held that Tamil songs were being denigrated somewhat by the penchant for Telugu and Sanskrit compositions (which were the main legacy of the great musical trinity of Tyagaraja, Muthuswami Dikshithar and Syama Sastri). The challenge to the domination of the Music Academy, which was largely Brahmin-centric, took the form of demanding a greater inclusion of Tamil in performances; this somewhat disguised its anti-Brahmin stance, although, to make the situation even more confusing, many prominent Brahmins such as Kalki Krishnamurthy and Rajaji supported the Tamil Isai Sangam. The Music Academy did itself no favours by resorting to ridiculous decisions such as the one where it boycotted M. S Subbulakshmi herself because she sang at one of the Sangam's early concerts. Regardless of the controversies and politics of competing sabhas, Carnatic music blossomed greatly between the 1930s and the 1960s in Chennai. The period was regarded as a golden era because of the great emphasis on individual styles and methods of singing; the emphasis was such that workshops as well as formal expositions became an integral part of the music season. This was of course an established tradition stemming from the Carnatic music 'duels' of the early years where virtuoso musicians, each with a large following, would challenge each other's expertise. Although such competitions do not exist today, many prominent musicians have a distinct idiom and method of performance with their own large fan bases. Apart from the prominent female musicians I have mentioned, any list of the great male vocalists of the past would have to include Chembai Vaidyanatha Bhagavathar, Ariyakudi Ramanuja Iyengar, Musiri Subramania Iyer, Semmangudi Srinivasa Iyer, G. N. Balasubramaniam and Madurai Mani Iyer. Additionally, there were extraordinarily accomplished veena players such as Chittibabu and Balachander; violinists such as T. N. Krishnan and percussion artists like Palghat Mani Iyer. In recent times, the western violin and even the saxophone have been introduced to the world of Carnatic music through brilliant exponents of the form like Lalgudi Jayaraman and Kadri Gopalnath.

The present generation of musicians beginning with the more senior vocalists such as Aruna Sairam, are P. Unnikrishnan, Sanjay Subrahmanyan, Nithyashree Mahadevan, Sudha Raghunathan, Bombay Jayashri (who was recently nominated for an Oscar for her song in the film *Life of Pi*) and T. M. Krishna. They have given Carnatic music new and exciting forms without sacrificing quality. Most of them are savvy, well educated, widely travelled and carry their genius lightly. While they are not weighed down by tradition, and certainly look far different from the traditional vidwans, they remain true to tradition in the larger sense and are often evangelical about it.

I speak to T. M. Krishna, who has just come from a cricket match with other young musicians. 'It's our way of relaxing after the rigours of the season. We have quite a team of players,' he smiles, as he rattles off the names of almost all of Chennai's more distinguished younger Carnatic musicians. 'And is your cricket as good as your music?' I ask. 'Probably,' he quips. Krishna's is a remarkable talent and the overflowing auditoriums and near stampedes at his performances attest to his popularity. His dream, however, was to become an economist and study at the London School of Economics, he says, although he'd always wanted to keep his music going. However, his musical ability was too good to be denied. He smiles as he remembers a concert in the main auditorium of the august Music Academy at the age of twelve. For one so young to have been encouraged to do this clearly indicated that there was something there that impelled a different kind of life response. Successive concerts made his career choice very clear, says Krishna, and after his college degree, he plunged into music, after which, of course, there was no looking back.

Krishna feels that however flawed the current sabha culture of Chennai is, it gives many young musicians the opportunity to hone their talents and slowly climb the ladder of accomplishment. 'The fact that you have many active musicians performing robustly in the forty-to-sixty age group as opposed to, say, the earlier generation which would be largely in the fifty-to-seventy age group indicates that Carnatic music has become younger; and interest is growing, with young people of our own generation being drawn to this. There is also a crossover to the film world—classical musicians sing in films without feeling compromised in any way,' he points out.

His friend and fellow musician Bombay Jayashri's Oscar nomination again underscores the intrinsic appeal of the music, whatever the platform. Krishna remarks that if by listening to the musical score in a film, someone is drawn to a classical music concert, then it's to the benefit of the musical tradition. 'There are two generations of young musicians waiting to succeed us and they come to Carnatic music from all over the globe,' he says. 'Chennai is the capital of the classical arts in this country,' he adds. 'The ability of people in the city to straddle many worlds and connect to every one of them is perhaps the most remarkable thing about the city.'

÷

Outside the world of classical music, is the tradition of gana paatu, originating with the fishing community and later infiltrating working class areas throughout the city. Gana paatu's themes typically turned social convention on its head, dealing with illicit relationships, alcohol and making fun of women. Some of them, on the other hand, also deify women and speak of love and longing. In many of these spontaneous folk expressions that are laced with both humour and cynicism, the layers of modern urban life are ripped to a rawness that sits uncomfortably wedged between its shining roads and flyovers, assuming a dark but sometimes redemptive life of its own. Amba paatu, another musical folk form of the fishermen, villu paatu, songs sung with locally made bows and other forms of folk music exist, but are not heard much outside the communities that foster them. By and large, Carnatic music along with film music, which these days tends to be a blend of western strains and melodies (often freely adapted) with some infusion of Indian or local elements, appear to be the two most popular musical forms in the city, especially among the young.

Another arena of entertainment in the city is theatre. Cho Ramaswamy's satirical plays, which he produced and often acted in, were very popular a couple of decades ago. Other well-known theatre luminaries of the past included Indira Parthasarathy, Pammal Sambanda Mudaliar, K. S. Nagarajan and N. Muthuswamy. Humour and slapstick, always popular with Chennai audiences, are abundant even today in the plays of S. Ve. Shekher, Crazy Mohan and others. According to filmmaker, theatre person and writer Prasanna Ramaswamy, however, 'The theatre of the sabhas, which we can call the spectacle tradition, has not really developed in new directions. There's a kind of tiredness and nothing really vibrant has emerged in recent times.'

Theatre in English is a long-standing Chennai

tradition—and amateur groups like the Madras Players consist of professionals working in diverse fields who band together seasonally to give the city some fine evenings of entertainment.

÷

Chennai's fame as one of the country's major centres of filmmaking began almost as soon as cinema first began. Mohan Raman, son of legal luminary V. P. Raman, is a film historian and television actor as well as a management consultant. He gives me a brief history of Indian cinema. '*Raja Harischandra* was the first film made by an Indian in India, in 1916 by Dadasaheb Phalke.' However, he tells me, movies came to India much earlier. 'Soon after cinema came to be in the West, a representative of the Lumière brothers travelled all over India in 1896 and showed film reels.' According to Mohan, a few years later, at the turn of the century, a man called Samikannu Vincent from Trichy, a former railway employee, 'bought a second-hand projector, a couple of reels of old films and started showing movies near Trichy. By 1910-1912 many theatres were built in Madras and three years after the first Indian film was made...Nataraja Mudaliar made the first film in Madras, at a place called Tower House on Millers Road off Poonamallee High Road.' Theatres such as the Gaiety, Roxy and Crown came into being, and new promoters like R. Venkaiyah and his son Prakash became involved with the movie business. Then there was A. Narayanan and his traditionally-dressed wife.

Mohan says, 'Here was this mami with a madisar boldly wielding a camera at the turn of the twentieth century.' These early filmmakers were succeeded by legendary names like K. Subramanyam and the multi-talented S. S. Vasan. On their watch, the Tamil film industry grew huge, the second largest in the country after Bollywood. Talented actors were discovered and fostered by men like Vasan who later took to directing as well. Gemini Studios, a few yards from the well-recognized city landmark Gemini flyover and the scene of many great movie productions, was built by him; the studio's entrance arch with the twin boys holding up their bugles was a familiar landmark. Vasan was also a journalist and launched the highly popular Tamil magazine *Ananda Vikatan*, which is still a favourite with many Chennai readers. B. Nagi Reddy who set up Vijaya Vauhini studios was another noted film producer in Chennai. He produced many highly-acclaimed films like *Patala Bhairavi*, *Missamma* and *Maya Bazaar*, and was given the Dadasaheb Phalke Award in 1987, Indian cinema's highest honour. He is also the founder of Vijaya Hospital, which, to this day, offers quality medical care at affordable costs. He started the highly popular children's magazine *Chandamama*, which delighted children of many generations with its engrossing tales from Indian mythology. In recent decades, directors like K. Balachander have taken Tamil cinema in new directions with hard-hitting unconventional themes, while younger directors like Mani Ratnam have been responsible for revolutionizing the Tamil movie industry with their use of story, cinematography and message. What is more, Mani Ratnam has garnered artistic success as well as critical commercial success.

Professor Stephen Hughes of the School of Oriental and African Studies (SOAS) who has studied the beginnings and growth of the cinema in Chennai, makes an interesting point: 'The development of public transportation [in Madras] roughly coincided with the growth and success of cinema exhibition... Both appeared in the public spaces of Madras as conspicuous signs of colonial modernity... Both opened up and institutionalized new kinds of public space which allowed for greater mixing at close proximity among those of different castes, classes and religious communities that would not normally interact.' This is an important insight: films in Chennai encouraged the growth of democratic space by being the great leveller especially at a time when caste and class rules were subtly in play, given that the lure and excitement of the movies appealed to all sections of society. And with the growth of public transport, the trams, buses and the occasional motorcar, going to the movies became a major pastime for the citizens of Chennai.

According to S. Muthiah, in an article called 'Cinema at Round Tana' the very first theatre that screened movies came up in 1911 on Popham's Broadway. It was called Bioscope and was owned by a Mrs Klug. However, it closed in a few months so the second theatre called the Electric owned by Warwick Major and Reginald Eyre is actually described as Madras's first cinema theatre. It began screening silent films in 1913. Other landmark cinemas that followed include the Elphinstone and the Wellington, both on Mount Road. These names were familiar to us in childhood, although by the time we grew up to become filmgoers it was the Safire Theatre that was the main magnet, a precursor to the present-day multiplexes.

÷

As young children we were of course not encouraged to see too many movies. If a film was reviewed well, especially if it was a period drama, we would be allowed to watch it. One such film, *Veerapandia Kattabomman*, which I saw some years after its original release when it played again in city theatres, made a deep impact on my young mind.

The film was based on the tragic story of the heroic Tamil chieftain of a small principality who defied the East India Company and was finally put to death by the British. It was brought splendidly to life by Sivaji Ganesan's memorable performance as Kattabomman. It won the actor international acclaim. All over the city, young and old would recite the various bits of memorable dialogue in the film; among the most declaimed lines (roughly translated here) were 'The skies shower and the earth bears, why should *you* get royalties? Why should *you* ask for tax?' Kattabomman thundered this at Jackson Thurai, the British agent. 'Did you come to our fields, did you water them, did you plant the paddy, pluck the weeds and carry the farmers' gruel? Did you grind turmeric and work for our young girls playing in these fields? Are you my uncle or my brother-in-law?' Many wept as they watched the film repeatedly during its long run in the city. As a result of the strong message in the film, my cousins and I temporarily became fierce Tamil nationalists.

Much before the advent of Sivaji and M. G. Ramachandran, M. K. Thyagaraja Bhagavathar was considered the first superstar of Tamil cinema. *Pavalakodi* was MKT's first film in 1934, followed by others like *Ambikapathy*, directed by Ellis Dungan, the American director who had an amazingly successful career during the early years of the Tamil film industry. I had the privilege to meet Dungan sometime in the 1990s at the house of my friend, the young filmmaker Chetan Shah. Chetan's parents knew Dungan during his Madras days in the 1950s before he left the city. Dungan must have been in his eighties on that visit to Chennai, but I recall that everyone at dinner was spellbound by his stories of the tantrums and idiosyncrasies of movie stars. Although Dungan had little technical expertise and no knowledge of the local language, he was remarkably successful in the nascent Tamil film industry. To go back to MKT, his story had a sad end, as along with another actor N. S. Krishnan, he was arrested in a famous murder case in the city. Although later acquitted, he lost interest in films and died in obscurity.

MGR, with his first great success *Sathi Leelavathi* (again directed by Dungan) became instantly popular. His other films like *Naadodi Mannan* and later *Rickshakaran*, which won him a national award, catapulted him to great cinematic heights and he was soon considered an icon in the city.

Sivaji Ganesan's genius lay in his versatility and superb dramatic talent. As I mentioned earlier, like in the *Kattabomman* film, he had an amazing ability to completely submerge himself in the characters that he portrayed. At least three generations of moviegoers in the city would weep over his character roles, recite his dialogues and rush to watch his every release. His work earned him many honours including the Dadasaheb Phalke Award. Male stars like Gemini Ganesan, Muthuraman, the genius comedian Nagesh and later, brilliant actors like Sivakumar (who is also a talented painter) kept the city's cinemagoers captivated as did many female stars beginning with Saroja Devi, Padmini, Savitri, K. R. Vijaya and later, J. Jayalalithaa. Suhasini Mani Ratnam, Revathi, and others are the next generation of actors who move effortlessly between television and films. They often write, direct and produce films and are also involved in a variety of causes outside the field of cinema.

The advent of male heroes like Kamal Haasan completely changed the face of the industry. While Kamal Haasan's many talents include screenwriting and directing, he is best known for his great versatility as an actor. His numerous film roles have won him national acclaim. In 1987, his role as the protagonist in Mani Ratnam's *Nayakan* was highly lauded; and it was listed by *Time* among the 100 best films of the world. But the energetic, vigorous, powerful and prolific world of Tamil cinema lives and breathes in the presence of an enormous backdrop, one of a towering man standing with arms crossed and legs apart. That man is the mega superstar Rajnikanth.

Rajnikanth, at sixty-three, is even today (despite occasional illness) one of the most revered and beloved icons of the Tamil people. After numerous box office hits and several flops as well, post the success of one of his recent films *Sivaji*, Rajnikanth is the second highest paid entertainer in Asia, next only to Jackie Chan. *Thalapathi*, directed by Mani Ratnam, *Chandramukhi*, *Enthiran* and *Muthu*, which had a huge fan following in Japan, are some of his great hits. *Newsweek* magazine commented that Rajnikanth had 'replaced Leonardo DiCaprio as Japan's trendiest heart throb'.

Rajnikanth, who since 1975 has enthralled audiences with more than 150 films, is revered as a godlike being by the citizenry of his hometown Chennai as well as the rest of Tamil Nadu. He has earned this status through the unique panache his screen characters always exude, one that incorporates flamboyant, confident language and trademark gestures of inimitable cool.

He further appeals to the public because of the roles he plays: he is often the champion of the oppressed and destroyer of the wicked. For instance, in *Sivaji* he plays a software specialist returning to Chennai from the US intent on contributing to the good of local society. His attempts to set up a college are thwarted by a powerful, crooked businessman with competing interests. Rajnikanth vanquishes him and saves the public from injustice.

Further enhancing his image are aspects of his personal life: he practices simplicity, his financial dealings are exemplary, he is deeply spiritual and, incredibly, he is not running for public office as is often the case with Tamil movie stars. All said and done, he is as important a feature of Chennai as the venerable Fort St George.

CHENNAI AT LEISURE

One morning, many years ago, I was suddenly summoned home from school, an extremely rare occurrence, I realized later, because at that age one is not much given to considering the circumstances that surround some of life's delicious moments. Nevertheless, although I have little memory of this, and only photographic proof, my time off from school was arranged so I could meet Sir Garfield Sobers, the great West Indian cricketer who had gained a reputation for all-round genius on the pitch. If the photograph is to be believed (the great man is smiling benignly in it) the meeting appeared to have gone well.

This is a cricket-mad city. The people of Chennai, across all ages, keenly follow test matches, one day cricket, IPL matches, league matches, club matches and even neighbourhood matches that are played by young boys on street corners. P. Subramanyam, a journalist based in the UK, remembers his childhood in Chennai in the mid-1940s, when even during the Second World War, with the city periodically gripped by the fear of bombing, the game of cricket went on. He recalls how in the immediate aftermath of peace, in 1945, the Australians came to play cricket in Madras. The team was made up of mostly ex-soldiers and servicemen on their way home to Australia after serving in the armies of Europe. Subramanyam remembers watching that match at the Chepauk Cricket Grounds as a youngster. 'Lala Amarnath made 113 and the young Parsi cricketer Rusi Modi made a stylish 203 not out. All of Madras was impressed with the Australians—captain Lindsay Hassett and Cecil Pepper, Keith Miller and John Pettiford,' recalls Subramanyam. In 1946, Subramanyam saw Denis Compton play for the Holkar XI in a Ranji Trophy match in Madras. 'After Denis Compton made 81 delectable runs, he was clean bowled by Madras speedster, C. R. Rangachari (a sub-inspector in the Madras Police from Triplicane) to the great joy of the Madras crowd. *The Hindu* published the picture of Compton being bowled, and overnight, the local boy became a celebrity. What's more, a little later the Triplicane police inspector went to play Test cricket in Australia, and made news again when he clean bowled the great Don Bradman!' says Subramanyam.

Chepauk Stadium, one of the iconic cricket match venues in India and adjacent to the Madras Cricket Club, has been witness to some spectacular matches. The city's first great cricketer was M. J. Gopalan, who according to the historian Ramachandra Guha, '...entered big cricket as a fast bowler, carrying his Iyengar caste marks of the namam (white paste, trident shaped, on forehead) and kudumi (pigtail) on to the cricket field. The namam was no hindrance, but as the kudumi would get loose while bowling, Gopalan invariably played with a close-fitting black cap'. Guha goes on to say that Gopalan 'rarely disappointed his admirers. One of his last flourishes was a hard-hitting half century as captain of the South Zone against the West Indies in 1949'.

Chennai has produced many great cricketers over the decades, including players who captained India like S. Venkataraghavan and Kris Srikkanth who was known to be a 'stylish opening batsman'. Srikkanth's exuberance and his 'swashbuckling' style always made the Chennai cricket crowd roar with delight whenever he walked on to the field. In the context of cricket, the spirit of the city is illustrated in a lovely anecdote briefly mentioned in an earlier chapter. Reporting on a historic India-Pakistan Test match in 1999, Qamar Ahmed wrote in *The Hindu*: 'Four days of intense cricket from either side and a sporting crowd to go with it, as the game took its twist and turn which made everyone feel for the players on both sides...although Pakistan won this sensational Test by a small margin, Indian cricket was not disgraced...Cricket has been done a favour by both teams and by the knowledgeable Chennai crowd who not only enjoyed every moment of it but also heartily cheered both the teams. Those who played and those who watched would surely remember this match for the rest of their lives. What was really most touching and emotional...was the response from the crowd when Pakistan dared to take a lap of honour to thank them. They greeted and cheered…and gave them a standing ovation.'

The Pakistan coach Javed Miandad and captain Wasim Akram both commended the 'splendid' Chennai crowd. A far cry from the chauvinism and bigotry of these days that seem to have become commonplace and often surface at other venues.

÷

Another great genius of Chennai is, of course, the master chess player Viswanathan Anand, the youngest Indian to win the title of International Grandmaster, whose accomplishments remain unmatched by anyone anywhere in India. A five-time winner of the World Chess Championship (the last in 2102), Anand began to play chess at the age of six, encouraged by his mother Susheela, who was something of a chess player herself. Anand recalls that during the brief period when he and his parents lived in the Philippines, and when he was still at school, his mother would note down chess games that she watched on television so that later they could solve them together. His great genius lies in his rapid moves and what is called his 'blitz' chess. Despite his stupendous achievements, Anand is known for his unassuming nature and has a reputation for refraining from psychological ploys while playing. He has also been called the 'Tiger of Madras'.

Tennis is another game that has placed the city of Chennai on the global sports map. The great first family of Indian tennis, T. K. Ramanathan, his son

Ramanathan Krishnan, and grandson Ramesh, played some of the most memorable tennis ever played in the country. For three generations our families have been friends, and when I recently visited Ramanathan Krishnan (now in his mid-seventies) I was struck not just by his passion for the game, but by the simplicity and elegance of thought and action that emanated from him, the hallmark of a person of exalted calibre. His charming wife Lalitha joins our conversation briefly, and tells me how under her father-in-law's tutelage she played against her son Ramesh and won many matches. Krishnan's humility is disarming; he tells me that the first shoes that he wore when he played tennis in Tenkasi as a young child, coached by his father T. K. Ramanathan, were made from worn out motorcycle tyres. T. K. Ramanathan, who was already ranked the No. 1 player in India, quickly saw the talent in his young son and moved the family to Madras in 1950 and worked tirelessly to train him.

Winning the Loyola College Cup when he was still a schoolboy after pleading and entreating with the authorities to admit him to a college-only tournament, (which Krishnan says they agreed to do because they were so fed up with him) he never looked back. He tells me about his trip by ship to England when he went to play at Wimbledon for the first time (he says he and his travelling companion yearned so much for Indian food that they completely emptied a jar of lime pickle and Mysore pak that they were carrying to deliver to someone else). He speaks of memorable matches and his great victories without a trace of pride; he won the Wimbledon Junior Championship, was India's first Wimbledon semi-finalist (twice) and went on to play spectacular matches during the Davis Cup tournaments.

Ramesh Krishnan, his son, continued in the great tradition of his father; apart from winning the Indian National Championship at the age of 16, he also won the US National Under-16 title, the only non-American to do so in 1977. Ramesh reached the quarter-final at Wimbledon and also twice reached the quarter-final of the US Open. Currently, both father and son focus on teaching tennis to children at the Krishnan Tennis Centre in the city.

The other brilliant tennis-playing multi-talented family from Chennai is of course the Amritraj family—brothers Vijay and Anand who reached the top echelons of tennis at Wimbledon and other tournaments including Grand Slams the world over. Vijay and Anand were doubles semi-finalists at Wimbledon in 1976, and ascended great heights of play. They were followed by Leander Paes, who also spent his formative years in Chennai.

÷

As Chennai was a city raised by the British, it is unsurprising that it is home to some legendary clubs. Among the oldest is the Madras Race Club. The history of racing in Madras goes back to 1777 but the club was only established in 1837. Fortunes have been gained and lost on its turf. There are other clubs in Chennai which are equally old. Indeed the Raj-era British thought of their clubs as an absolute necessity, a refuge to which they could retreat after a hard day's work dealing with bewildering natives. These clubs offered them pastimes revered in their homeland, including but not limited to hunting, betting at the Epsom Derby (which was relayed by radio), serious drinking and inexpensive, colonial-style dining. The Madras Club, founded in 1832, moved from location to location before settling in its present space with the magnificent Moubray's Cupola as its centrepiece. Sir Henry Chamier, after whom one of the city's premier connecting roads is named, was the club's first president. It was initially an all-white, all male preserve until, as V. Sriram tells me, 'it came down to just one Englishman' and Indians were hastily admitted. The Gymkhana Club, founded in 1884, was 'a gentleman's club' with its membership largely drawn from the Madras garrison, the colonial elite and some highly connected Indians.

Typical of these clubs were extensive grounds, a handsome main building or clubhouse that would comprise a large smoking lounge with ancient chairs (some upholstered with rivet-studded leather); a bar fashioned out of fine wood, like teak or rosewood; a dining hall where diners were attended on by white-gloved, turbaned waiters; a billiards saloon and a card-room for those who wanted to indulge in some serious gambling. As time went by, swimming pools, gyms and tennis courts were inevitably put in; and, as even more time went by, the membership transitioned from pure white to almost totally brown.

Other notable clubs of British origin are the Cosmopolitan Club and the Madras Cricket Club (MCC). All much sought-after, present-day characteristics common to all of them include exorbitant entry fees, limited membership quotas, endless waiting lists and, very important to many, exclusive status.

As a result of the huge demand for club membership, fresh clubs constantly spring up, notable examples being the Presidency Club and the Gandhi Nagar Club. All said and done, these clubs are perceived as being crucial for maintaining a healthy social circulation within the city.

÷

Public spaces in Chennai have an interesting history beginning with colonial notions of the sort of civic amenities that would be good for the 'natives', while making sure the white population was not inconvenienced in the least. A. Srivathsan wrote a perceptive essay on the British attempts to 'educate' the people through the creation of public spaces like the Esplanade Maidan and the People's Park, while ignoring their traditional methods of socializing and interacting with each other in bazaars and temples. He recounts an 1880 sketch of native life that 'amusingly narrates the penchant of a well-dressed native for horse rides in the new urban spaces like the Bandstand Promenade, South Beach and People's Park, only to come back in time in the evening for a trip to the temple with his family in a dhoti and then quietly slip to the Dambachari [one of the first social plays in Tamil] and "nautch girl" performances in the night'.

While markets and temples continue to serve as spaces where people connect with neighbours and friends, the notion of sitting in parks and planted gardens did gradually gain popularity. The former Mayor of Chennai, Maa. Subramaniam, told me that in the earlier regime, where public lands were encroached upon by private parties (to the extent of several thousand crores of rupees in value) they were mostly retrieved, and parks and playgrounds were created for public use.

However, there is one recreational place that dwarfs all the others. Free, and still beautiful in places, the beaches that border the Bay of Bengal provide the city's residents with a clear view of the horizon, where the sky and sea meet and it appears as if there is nothing beyond.

Marina Beach could well be the best-known jewel in Chennai's motley crown. One of my earliest memories of Marina Beach is the grey sand between my toes, and the small wriggling crabs that terrified me as I stood at the water's edge clutching an adult hand. Although the crabs usually minded their own business and, at my approach, would scurry swiftly down their perfectly formed bolt-holes deep in the sand, I found them menacing.

Even now, every Friday, Saturday and Sunday evening, Chennai families swarm towards Marina Beach in cars and motorcycles and on foot. They go because, among other things, this is one place in Chennai where, with the sea breeze on your face and nothing between you and the ocean, in spite of everything around you—the crowds, the dirt, the noise—it is possible to feel at peace.

The beach isn't always clean, and as the municipal authorities haven't provided enough garbage cans, the crowds of beachgoers leave behind thousands of kilograms of wrapping paper, plastic bags, styrofoam cartons and similar litter every evening. After decades of indifference, the city authorities decided a clean beach might be an improvement upon a garbage-strewn one. They appointed a small army of trash pickers who, every morning, sweep across the beach like a 500-foot-wide vacuum cleaner. All garbage that meets the eye is removed, readying the beach for the next onslaught of abuse.

In earlier days, the beach was lined with a mere tar road. At the tail end of the twentieth century, however, the city authorities decided to add some spit and polish. Stainless steel railings were constructed and a proper road led on to the beach with spacious parking areas attached to it. At one time, a garden restaurant materialized near the long-standing statue of Mahatma Gandhi. It seemed a bit incongruous, but it disappeared soon enough, and today, while there are no restaurants to block the view of the sea, you can still find food carts whose wares only the bravest venture to sample.

When our children were young we decided that they too needed the beach experience as a formative influence in their lives much as it had been in ours. To be honest,

I'm not sure that was the only reason we took our children down to the beach—those visits may have simply been an excuse to let the young ones burn off excess energy, and give us some respite from the joys of parenthood. I remember one particular evening there was a small but conspicuous group of men in their white dhotis surrounding two or three people sitting on the sand. I recognized our chief minister as being among their number. In those days the security surrounding such dignitaries was much more relaxed. I pointed him out to the children.

'Can I go and speak to him?' my older son asked. He must have been six or seven years old.

'Well, you can try,' I said, ever eager to test people's power at the grassroots.

'Hello,' said my son holding his hand out to the Chief Minister, 'my name is Narayan.'

'Hello,' said the Chief Minister, 'my name is Karunanidhi.'

÷

And now, to that other great pastime of the citizens of Chennai: food. As in the case of most cities which have existed for hundreds of years, Chennai's food is a distinct and very important part of its character. One can assume that the earliest food relished by the city's inhabitants was based almost entirely on local produce such as rice, lentils, tamarind, fish, mutton, chicken, tomatoes, eggplant, ladies' fingers, carrot, cucumber, beans, pumpkin, raw banana and yam. Later on, after the advent of the British, came that saving grace of humankind, the potato.

From a selection of the above (vegetarian) ingredients a lentil stew called sambar was made, which was eaten along with rice. A variation of this was called rasam; this was lighter, more fragrant and soup-like in its attributes. The typical vegetarian Chennai spread would comprise rice with sambar followed by rice with rasam, and spicy cooked vegetables on the side. The vegetables and extras would be prepared in special ways by different communities. For example, a mild, non-onion, non-garlic, mildly spiced version would be typical of Tamil Brahmin fare, while a more racy onion and garlic-imbued version would be made by the Chettiars; the Andhras of Chennai would liberally flavour their vegetables with hot red and green chilis; inevitably, all these meals would be completed with rice and buttermilk or curd. This type of meal was called ellai sappaadu, meaning a 'meal on leaves' as they were typically eaten on banana leaves. But these full-on meals aside, traditionally Chennaites would also eat light meals known as tiffin. One noteworthy tiffin dish is the idli, which is mostly eaten at breakfast. The idli has a renowned sibling: the dosai, ('dosa' to the tragically uninitiated); other tiffin staples include the vadai and bonda. Kerala has contributed the puttu, appam and idiappam, Karnataka has introduced Chennaites to bisibele bath and vaangi bath, and the Telugu's best-known tiffin foods are the pesarattu, and of course the fiery pickles that accompany most meals.

Today, well-known North Indian foods like chapattis, naan and pooris have made their way into Chennai households. It is possible to find traditional Rajasthani, Gujarati and other non-indigenous fare like rich badam milk, fried onion kachoris, gol guppas and the more universal tikkis and chaats in eateries on Mint Street and Elephant Gate.

÷

As the city of Chennai grew in economic activity, it often became necessary for people to leave home for work early in the morning and return late in the evening, making it inconvenient to eat at home. This led to a strong demand for restaurants. The oldest vegetarian restaurants appeared in the oldest part of the city—George Town. Ramakrishna Lunch Home is one such example. Further south, in Triplicane is Ratna Café (where 'café' is pronounced 'cayf'), where, to this day, waiters will give you as much sambar as you ask for, pouring it onto your plate from a stainless steel mug (which is not done anywhere else).

Somewhat nearby in the Mylapore area, along the banks of the once grand waterway called the Buckingham Canal, was a small cubbyhole of a restaurant called Rayar Café (Rayar 'Cayf', of course), renowned for its tiffin. Although it was remarkably dark and cave-like, weekend mornings would see lines of parked cars choking Kutchery Road, the approach to Rayar Café.

These cars, surprisingly, belonged to North Indian

residents of Chennai indulging their weekly breakfast fix of traditional Tamil food. Sadly, the café fell on bad times and had to move, although the original owners' family still runs it. Currently, it is located in more modest surroundings off Kutchery Road and although its glory days are long past, it still attracts regulars like Cho Ramaswamy, the famous writer, editor, satirist and critic. Another favourite of Mylapore residents is the Karpagambal Mess which has been popular since the early 1950s, especially with vegetarian tiffin lovers. The owner is a devout man who swears that his business's success is entirely because of the family's multi-generational devotion to Lord Kapaliswara whose abode is across the road from this eatery. Their pongal is reputed to be heavenly and the variety of vadai on offer is quite astounding. They are famous for their ghee-dripping badam halva and the array of sweets in a glass counter near the entrance is enough to make one feel faint from an imagined sugar high. The walls are filled with pictures of Gods and Goddesses who look benignly down on the diners, probably keeping a watchful eye in case someone gets into trouble with such rich food around; the owner proudly tells me of the huge quantities of ghee used each day in their food, especially the halvas and other sweets.

Apart from the restaurants just mentioned, there are two other hotels with attached restaurants which are famous for their vegetarian food: Dasaprakash and Woodlands, both founded by dirt-poor young boys who came to this city from a region hundreds of miles away which is famous for its food—Udupi in the neighbouring state of Karnataka.

The Saravana Bhavan chain of restaurants has branched out prolifically into all the major boroughs of Chennai, and maintains a consistent quality of food and service at each outlet. The founder is obviously a savvy entrepreneur, since he has not limited himself to Chennai—there are now Saravana Bhavans in Dubai, Singapore, and perhaps not very surprisingly, in Silicon Valley as well (with more than two hundred reviews on Zagat to boot).

Non-vegetarians have their own favourites. Once, the ubiquitous 'military' hotel could be found all over the city—no-frills establishments where diners were served low-cost, surprisingly tasty food—biryani with half a boiled egg perched on a mound of deliciously spiced rice threaded with browned onions and well-cooked meat; thick, aromatic chicken and mutton curries; and fish and prawn flavoured with coconut. One of the most famous of these establishments is Ponnusamy, famous for its crab, fish and biryanis. It grew so successful that it opened branches, including an upscale one in Egmore, and is perhaps as famous as Buhari—founded by a Sri Lankan immigrant. Its best-known product is Chicken 65—spicy, batter-coated chicken nuggets, but it is also famous for its biryanis, Malabar parathas, and mutton and chicken kormas.

Another little-known food specialty comes from an unexpected quarter—the many temples that make daily offerings of food to their deities. The temple authorities and priests fill huge vats with the fragrant food and distribute it free of cost as prasadam; this is consumed not just by the devotees who come to worship, but all manner of locals, a significant proportion of whom rely on it for regular sustenance. Amazingly, despite the sometimes large quantities that are cooked, the food remains distinctly aromatic and fresh even hours after preparation. In the context of the offerings made in temples in Chennai, also called naivaidyam (it is only called prasadam when distributed to devotees), my friend Prasanna Ramaswamy says that apart from the delicious chakkara pongal at the Triplicane Temple, the cashewnut vadai is a delicious but lesser-known specialty. 'In Siva temples like Kapaliswara, on certain festival days in the month, a variety of offerings ranging from marukozhundu and dhawanam mix (fragrant herbs used in flower garlands) to sugar, milk and curd are applied on Lord Kapali and then distributed to the public. The other deities too have their specialty offerings, such as sesame seasoned rice. They are all cooked in very special ways,' she says.

With the liberalization of the Indian economy, several international food chains have set up shop in the city, as they have done elsewhere in the country—Pizza Hut, KFC, McDonalds, Dominos, are all popular with Chennaites, especially the young. More interesting than these are specialty restaurants set up by entrepreneurs of Indian origin who have returned to the city after long years in the US and elsewhere. One example is Amadora. Owner Deepak Suresh, after spending several decades in Boston, has come back to Chennai to run a gourmet ice cream shop. Deepak says that, except for the cocoa, all the ingredients originate in India, thus disproving the popular notion that quality food ingredients are not available in India. He recounts how some customers from Europe had marvelled at his peanut butter ice cream and asked him which American brand of peanut butter he was using. They were surprised when he told them that it was from Kerala!

DEGREE COFFEE BY THE YARD

Coffee was a big deal in my family, especially in my mother's family. They moved to Madras from Thanjavur in the fifties and brought with them a passion for coffee along with a propensity for intellectual pursuits, politics, lengthy discussions on philosophy as well as all manner of public affairs—these were mostly habits acquired from my grandfather who was deeply involved in the freedom movement and in Gandhian politics. When he moved his family to Madras they also brought with them coffee-making skills that visitors to their home felt were unmatched. I remember sentiments like 'Coffeekku vazhi unda?' which translates to 'Is there a pathway to coffee?' floating around the house as if the beverage were the path to enlightenment. It seemed to me, as a child visiting my grandparents, that there were always tumblers of strong, delicious coffee available at all times of the day; sweet enough for a child sometimes, and at other times strongly brewed and dark like some sinister drink that would at once bestow special powers on the drinker. My mother, a coffee aficionado herself, feared that her children would also succumb to coffee's allure, so while we were allowed to inhale the aroma, we were not permitted to drink the litres of coffee that were brewed each day.

At four o'clock the milkman or paalkaran would appear at my grandfather's gate with his doleful looking cow and would call out to the household to witness the milking and transfer of the milk from the cow's udders into the container—which had to be examined to ensure that there was no water already in it to dilute it. This was cow's milk, but he also sold buffalo's milk and my grandmother was vague about which creature's milk actually went into the coffee. Of course there were the inevitable heated discussions between my uncles and grandfather about which milk worked best (buffalo's milk was the right answer, impossible to get in the city nowadays) but I really doubt whether they had a choice in the matter, because the making of the coffee was the preserve of my serene and gentle grandmother who was as tough as steel on things that mattered to her. When we were old enough (my mother ruled that we had to be twelve years old at least before we were allowed our first cup of coffee and it was of course restricted to one cup a day for a while), we took great glee in actually handling the customary tumbler and dabara (a wide saucer with high sides) from which the coffee was drunk because it felt like a very grown-up thing to do. Our greatest delight was to raise our tumblers high and pour the hot liquid into the dabara from as great a height as we could manage in order to cool it sufficiently so it could be drunk. This movement up and down, transferring the coffee from dabara to tumbler and back would also enhance the frothiness of the drink. There was some competition among the cousins who gathered on weekends at our grandparents' place as to who could pour from the greatest height without spilling any of it. Inevitably, there were accidents, and grown-up reactions to these ranged from patient tolerance (and even a little admiration perhaps for a child acquiring a new and useful skill) to irritation at having to clean up the mess. Another intriguing challenge had to do with drinking coffee from a silver tumbler which was shaped like a tapered beaker. You had to pour the hot beverage directly into your mouth without your lips touching the rim. I never quite got the point of drinking coffee this way because the metal tumbler (usually made of silver or sometimes of stainless steel) would be hot to the touch which would in itself be uncomfortable; add to that, the not very happy experience of pouring boiling coffee down your throat, and it wasn't something that made much sense to me. A. R. Venkatachalapathy, in his essay on coffee, has drawn an observation from the well-known Tamil writer A. K. Chettiar who says that 'the widespread use of metal tumblers with rims, unlike the rimless North Indian ones is a Tamil (Brahmin) invention, enabling the drinking of coffee without sipping the tumbler, it facilitated the balancing of hospitality and avoiding ritual pollution.' Of course one was not aware of these sociological implications as a child. What existed was just the thrill of the operation with a beverage that seemed to have magical powers.

Coffee was frequently a topic of discussion in my mother's family. This ranged from the variety of theories and lore about its origins and its international appeal down to discussing the best blend of coffee beans for that perfect mix. Such conversations would not actually happen while the coffee was being drunk, as usually there were some reverential moments of silence when the coffee appeared. But after that initial moment of communion with the god of coffee, I remember many memorable conversations that revolved around the beverage.

My mother's early years of marriage in a joint family did not give her the luxury of importing the secret of her own family's mastery of coffee into her new domain, and it was only later on, when she ran her own household, that she gave me her special coffee powder formula, variations of which I believe are prevalent in many households in Chennai today. Robusta beans or Plantation A combined with Peaberry beans, freshly ground and mixed to the formula of 1:3, was what she prescribed. Plantation A was more frequently used in the mix as Robusta was not always available. Robusta (or its substitute Plantation A) gave the decoction its body. Peaberry gave the best flavour, my mother said. Robusta A and Peaberry Special was however the ideal combination, in her opinion. A dash of chicory, which gave coffee its strong flavour, according to her, was also an ingredient in some coffees (especially in readymade powders), but the Peaberry-Plantation A was 'our house formula'. I carried on the tradition and do believe that we produce decent enough coffee in our home.

Ever since its first appearance when it began to replace neeragaram (kanji or gruel made from fermented rice water from a previous meal, with added spices) the city has been captivated by coffee. Although Venkatachalapathy speaks of 'an initial cultural' anxiety when coffee first appeared, 'matched only by the enthusiasm by which it was consumed', this sense of ambivalence seems to have vanished quickly. In its subsequent spread through the city, methods of making coffee have grown in multiple ways. However, the most traditional Chennai coffee filter is a unique metal contraption, and while fairly simple in construction, demands a particular skill in the way in which it is used. This stainless steel coffee filter is in two parts of almost equal halves. The bottom of the top container is perforated and the powder is measured into this top half. There is also a pressing disc with a stem that holds down (but sometimes shakes, so has to be carefully handled) the coffee powder. When boiling water is poured into the top container, one must ensure that the stem does not shake or tip over but is stable, and then the lid is carefully placed on top to keep in the aroma while the liquid decoction slowly drips into the bottom container. Once the coffee decoction drips down to the bottom container fully, it is likely to be strong, dark and full-bodied (unlike the much more dilute decoction that emerges from coffee makers) and thought to have the best flavour. In most households, boiling water is poured a second time on the same powder, in order to extract a more dilute blend of the decoction. This is usually meant for children or for others who are more fragile in the pecking order of consumption. Hot frothy milk and sugar are added to the decoction and, as mentioned earlier, through dexterous arm movements that involve pouring the coffee from a particular height between the tumbler and dabara (almost as if one were measuring yardage) the coffee is cooled to the desired amount. Another name for this pure filter coffee is 'metre' coffee, probably derived from the distance between the dabara and the tumbler when the coffee is being cooled.

÷

In many homes in Chennai the first thing they will ask you when you visit is: 'Would you like a cup of coffee?' If you demur, you will hear one or all of the following: 'Just half a tumbler at least?' or 'We have a secret formula' or 'Do try our special coffee' and many such adumbrations that are supposed to tempt you to immediately agree to try that special coffee. It is often considered inhospitable if you are not plied with coffee the moment you enter a Chennai house. Tea, on the other hand, while growing in popularity, including the newer formulations like peppermint, camomile and green tea, somehow does not seem to be able to dislodge coffee as the all-time favourite drink in Chennai. The master novelist R. K. Narayan, who lived for many years in the city, was a great votary of the beverage. He wrote: '[Coffee] is not a habit; it is a stabilizing force in human existence achieved through a long evolutionary process.' In an essay, charmingly titled 'Coffee Worries' which appeared in 1974, he points out that 'For a South Indian, of all worries the least tolerable is coffee worry...[which] may be defined as all unhappy speculation around the subject of coffee as a habit, its supplies, its price, its quality, its morality, its ethics, economics and so on'. Narayan suggests that the coffee drinker whose habit is criticized will probably view it 'as an attack on his liberty of thought and action'. He emphasizes that 'all the moralizing against coffee has misfired in this part of the country. "Coffee is a deadly poison, you are gradually destroying your system with it, etc.," declares some purist. He may lecture from a public platform or on a street corner but people will listen to him only with a pitying tolerance, with an air of saying, "Poor fellow, you don't know what you are talking about, you don't know what you are missing. You will still live and learn". In course of time this prophecy is fulfilled', says Narayan. 'Many a man who has come to scoff has remained to pray. Coffee has many conquests: saints, philosophers, thinkers and artists who can never leave the bed unless they learn that coffee is ready, but not the least of its conquests is among those who came to wage a war on it.'

The writer Asokamitran explained to me that 'degree coffee' probably meant a particularly high quality of milk that was used in Kumbakonam and thereafter popularized in Chennai. Another explanation is that 'chicory' came to be pronounced as 'degree' and yet another elucidation of the term is that degree coffee usually stands for the undiluted, strong-bodied decoction that is first filtered. While traditional coffee making is said to be somewhat on the decline given the increasing pace of life in Chennai, a range of people that I enquired with indicated that they still made filter coffee regularly; 'instant' coffee was reserved for unexpected guests or when there were other compelling reasons for not decocting proper coffee.

For Chennai's coffee enthusiasts, there is now an immense amount of choice as lattes, cappuccinos, espressos and macchiatos brewed by a variety of chains battle it out for primacy with purveyors of the traditional filter coffee. For now, at any rate, the overwhelming majority of the city's residents that I spoke to favour the traditional brew. And the search for that perfectly brewed cup of coffee remains one of the city's obsessions.

As a true Chennai vasi, I too am always on the trail of that perfect cup and although I cannot always find it, I can recognize it when I taste it.

IN THE END, THE BEGINNING

When I began this book, I sought the advice of the writer Asokamitran on how I might capture the essence of the city. He wisely said: 'Start with your area, your locality, if you want to write about the city.' Although I did not quite begin like that, my origins and rootedness in Chennai were always at the back of my mind. Further, I will concede, Alwarpet, where I grew up, provided me with the passport to begin my journey. As Asokamitran reminded me, my place of origin in the city was one that was especially vivid in my mind. It had broad roads with garden houses, old temples tucked into small streets, and was home to entrepreneurs, lawyers, successful filmmakers, pioneering physicians, scientists and scholars; at one time, even a former President of India, Sarvepalli Radhakrishnan, lived at the border of Alwarpet. The only locality without a statue, Asokamitran pointed out, with a twinkle. And that says much in a city that is drawn to myth-making and statue-building that in turn creates heroes.

In the days of my youth, vast expanses of green rice fields, banana trees, coconut groves and jasmine gardens formed the backdrop to most of the city. Those were slower times in Madras, when people had the time to tell us stories, did interesting jobs like climbing coconut trees and catching snakes and could simply pass the time sitting on creaky wooden swings on ancient verandahs. Growing up in such a milieu you acquired an all-round education, unlike the 'lite education' (as my friend Radha Hegde calls it) which is available these days. Radha shares memories of growing up in Alwarpet, Chennai. She and her sisters would stroll on roads filled with white blossoms that went 'pop-pop' when they walked on them. Her old family home is now an apartment complex; close by, she notes 'are pizza parlours, consulates, software offices, symbols of global mobility'. She is struck by the neo-liberal packaging of Chennai as a global city. Tradition is now adapted and made portable, she points out, such as in shops like Giri Trading Agency in Luz which offers a moveable, plastic version of Hinduism for today's consumer.

Like other cities of India, Chennai now has malls and coffee shops with branded goods and services. There is a uniformity that blurs the contours of an older city. Young people group together in these places and discuss the latest films, make plans to go to America or Australia and, of course, debate whether it is time to disclose the presence of the boyfriend or girlfriend to their parents. Nevertheless, despite their twenty-first-century obsessions, they tell me they are proud to belong to the city and like its unique ways. In Chennai, it is not surprising to see young girls in tees and jeans emerging from a visit to the temple with strands of jasmine precariously affixed to short cropped hair. Nor is it unusual to see teenage girls in hijabs, laughing as they fly by on their scooters on the way to college. Or an enterprising flower vendor whisk out a calculator or a mobile phone. The old men still find the beach salubrious enough for their morning constitutionals. Despite the chain stores and air-conditioned fruit and vegetable shops, many of the city's residents still prefer to go to the traditional bazaars or buy their produce from the itinerant vendors with their wares perched on their heads. *The Hindu* is still loved and read. Music fills the air in and out of season, the call of the muezzin is still heard; on Sundays the churches are filled with people. We all read the (now digital) messages on church boards when we drive by, hoping of course for a sign that we are on the right track.

This is the city of the fisherfolk as much as it is the city of old Marwari families in George Town; the city of the aging padre cycling down Santhome's quiet bylanes, of children laughing as they play street cricket, and of the young businesswoman who steps into her gleaming glass and chrome twenty-first-century office every morning. It is a city where peacocks still dance just as they did two thousand years ago, where people still trade and build as they once did, fight and pray as they always have. It is a city where people continue to make and lose fortunes, live and die in the name of causes they believe in and a place where they read and write books, compose songs, act, make movies, dream dreams and fashion lives among its ancient stones as well as its shining new roadways.

Jeffrey Hawkins, an American diplomat, who lived in Chennai in the 1990s wrote to me about his memories of the city: 'I had an elephant living on my street. After I left Madras and wanted to share the wonder and magic of the place, that elephant was often the symbol I used. Part Ganesh, part bristly grey sage, I was always enchanted by his stately presence. At certain times of the year, great old flowering trees would blossom on Boat Club Road. The street would be densely carpeted with purple blossoms. On my steamy, misty, early morning runs I would sometimes be overwhelmed with a sense that a god had passed that instant, leaving a bed of flowers in his wake.'

The city that is magical for some is a battleground for others. I cannot forget Gnanasekaran, the fisherman, who lives in a tiny tin-roofed house by the Bay of Bengal with his wife, and two daughters whom he struggles to educate. His dream is to own his own mechanized boat and to live in an environment that will not just keep his girls safe but will pilot them to a secure adulthood. Chennai, like many other cities, is rife with disparities, with disaffection; flowers adorn footpaths while impoverished families wonder if they will survive another day. However, given the testimonies of endurance and voices of hope that I heard, I am reassured that this city will carry on.

÷

degree coffee by the yard

Sushila Ravindranath tells me how she, along with the city's premier historians S. Muthiah, V. Sriram and others like Vincent D'Souza, put together a Madras Week every year, and other festivals to celebrate the city through stories, talks and walks that are free and inclusive. 'It's a mixture of nostalgia, entertainment and what is happening now. It seems to have taken on a life of its own with schools and associations jumping in and participating. And it's all about this city. We have talks about old doctors and old lawyers. Television actor Mohan Raman speaks about Sivaji Ganesan, danseuse Anita Ratnam demonstrates modern dance, 'Tennis' Krishnan speaks tennis of course. We also have young entrepreneurs speaking about their experiences in the city. The response is growing staggeringly every year,' she says.

So the people of Chennai not only want to understand their city, but themselves too. Amidst the colour and confusion is a deeply felt sense of belonging which I heard in all the stories that were told to me. This city is like the coffee it brews and drinks: degree coffee—rich, full-bodied and beneath the surface of the foaming hot milk, a substance that keeps your pulse racing.

Gopalkrishna Gandhi once wrote memorably about the city, 'It is about what we receive here, what we are given…'

He goes on to say: 'Whenever I see a woman washing her tiny vaasal-padi and then on that small surface, despite cares and anxieties, ill-health and a demanding day ahead of her, draw an amazing kolam, I offer her an invisible namaskaram. Perhaps the Euclidean balance of dots and loops, lines and curves on that little drawing give her the inner balance that life denies her…'

For me too it is about what I receive here, what I am given. Chennai is home, and as T.S. Eliot wrote, 'Home is where one starts from'.

ACKNOWLEDGEMENTS

This book owes everything to the city I write about. To its people, its traditions and its extraordinary spirit exemplified through the lives of the men and women I've known and met, especially in the course of writing this book. The book exists because of them and to them I owe my deepest gratitude.

My grateful thanks are first to my editor and long-time friend David Davidar who startled me with the idea when he wanted me to join the group of illustrious writers who were writing a city series for him. The faith he reposed in me, and his confidence that I could capture the essence of the city in a short book encouraged me hugely. For that I am deeply grateful. My thanks are many to Pujitha Krishnan, my editor at Aleph, whose skills sharpened my manuscript. I appreciate all the time and trouble she took over the book. I am very grateful too to Aienla Ozukum for steering me gently through the various stages of production of this book.

To S. Muthiah, Madras/Chennai's foremost chronicler, who set the stage for recording this city's history and whose contributions to its heritage are vast and immeasurable, I owe much. Beyond his particular encouragement and ideas for this book, I have also used considerable information and material from his already published works. Over the years he has also been a mentor and a kind friend; he has always inspired me with his energy and with the immense range and depth of his knowledge of this city and much more.

I am also greatly indebted to my friend V. Sriram, historian, writer, businessman and specialist in music, who pointed me in the direction of experts and research material on the city. He patiently spent many evenings with me talking 'heritage', and as we wandered through the city, helped me see it in a light that was both enchanting and illuminating. Sushila Ravindranath, journalist and old friend often kept us company, gave me many ideas and constantly supported me as I was writing the book.

I am grateful to Asokamitran, the venerable writer whose knowledge about Chennai and sharp observations about the nature of its people gave me much to think about. I thank S. Anvar for enlightening conversations, for his unstinting generosity in terms of the time he spent with me offering new and invaluable insights that I could not have really found in the pages of any book. The historian Dr Chithra Madhavan liberally and unhesitatingly shared her knowledge and expertise over many hours of conversation, and my grateful thanks to her. Special thanks are due to my friend Prasanna Ramaswamy who shared some interesting perspectives and was a great source of encouragement.

Dr A. Srivathsan, Associate Editor, *The Hindu*, helped me begin this journey suggesting new ways of looking at the city. My thanks to him and very special thanks to Dr A. R. Venkatachalapathy, historian nonpareil and dear friend, whose conversations about the city opened up new vistas and perspectives, many of which I still need to explore. I have not really been able to do justice to many of the concerns that he and I discussed, and hope that future histories of the city will include some of those perspectives in more detail than I have been able to. Special thanks are due to my very dear friend Dr Radha Hegde, Associate Professor of Media, Culture, and Communication, New York University, who gave me valuable suggestions for this book. Her penetrating insights and depth of perspective about the city that she grew up in greatly enhanced my approach to the subject. Thanks too to my old friend Jeff Hawkins for his contribution and for cheer from afar.

To B. Kolappan, Senior Assistant Editor, *The Hindu*, Deepa Ramakrishnan, Special Correspondent, *The Hindu*, Aloysius Xavier Lopez, Principal Correspondent, *The Hindu*, I convey my thanks for the help they extended. Their connect to the city is remarkable and I benefitted greatly from their resourcefulness.

The following people generously shared their time and insights and I owe them a deep debt of gratitude: In alphabetical order, R. Azhagarasan, Bablu Thomas, K. Badrinath, Chitra Mahesh, Dhanalakshmi, Gnanasekaran, Gopalkrishna Gandhi, R. Kannan, Kiran Rao, B. A. Kodandaraman, P. T. Krishnan,

P. Kumar, Lakshmi Vishwanathan, K. Mani, Mohan Raman, K. Moortheeswari, Nalli Kuppuswami Chetti, Neeti Anil Kumar, S. Prabhudas, G. Ramakrishnan, Randor Guy, Ranjitha Ashok, Rita Chaudhuri, Rohini, Senapathy Sivachariar, K. V. Srinivasan, actor P. Sivakumar, S. Sivakumar, Maa Subramanian, P. Subramanyam, S. Venkatraam and Vidya Singh.

I could not have done the research and interviews without the help of K. N. Parthasarathy, *The Hindu*, who facilitated and supported much of the background work. My thanks are also due to R. Ramesh, *The Hindu*. I would like to convey my thanks and appreciation to the Archives Department of *The Hindu* for their support and input.

My mother, Menaka Parthasarathy, was not only a source of constant inspiration and encouragement, but shared her memories of the city, our family, and helped to translate material in Tamil for my use. And finally, I could not have written this book without my stern in-house editor Lakshman Balaraman whose clarity of thought, rigorous editing skills and constant pushing helped me to finally get it done.

My thanks are also due to many others in Chennai, family and friends (they know who they are) who gave me time, pointed me in new directions and helped me better understand the city that we all love.

The poem 'Madras' in the epigraph is quoted with permission from the poet Arundhati Subramaniam.

The extract from 'Coffee Worries' by R. K. Narayan is reproduced with permission from the Legal Heirs of R. K. Narayan.

The extract from 'Chennai is us, its residents' is quoted with permission from Gopalkrishna Gandhi.

The extract from 'Madras Mannade' is quoted with permission from Dr A. R. Venkatachalapathy.

The extract from the article 'The Days With Bharathi' by N. Ramaswami Iyer is quoted with permission from N. R. Chandran.

NOTES

REFLECTIONS OF A CHENNAI VASI

3 'a way of looking at life': Orhan Pamuk, *Istanbul: Memories Of A City* (London: Faber and Faber 2005) p. 82.

6 'colonial': A. R. Venkatachalapathy (ed.), *Chennai Not Madras: Perspectives on the City* (Mumbai: Marg Publications, 2006) p. 4.

6 'unsung yet glorious': Ibid.

11 'goal': E. B. White, *Here is New York* (New York: The Little Bookroom, 1976) p. 26.

11 'final destination': Ibid.

11 'in quest of something': Ibid.

11 'its incomparable achievements': Ibid.

13 'being of a shy and retiring disposition': V. K. Narasimhan, *Builders of Modern India—Kasturi Ranga Iyengar* (New Delhi: Publication Division, Ministry of Information and Broadcasting, Government of India, 1963) p. 12.

14 'by the turn of the twentieth century': A. R. Venkatachalapathy, *In Those Days There Was No Coffee—Writings in Cultural History—New Perspectives on Indian Pasts* (New Delhi : Yoda Press 2006) p. 27.

14 'I never tire of': Ibid., p. 28.

THE STORY OF MADRAS

17 a small sarcophagus: K. V. Raman, *The Early History of the Madras Region* (Chennai: Amudha Nilayam, 1959) p. 22.

17 'Mylarphon': *The Madras Tercentenary Commemoration Volume* (Madras: Humphrey Milford Oxford University Press, 1939) p. 41. Also see K. Kalpana and Frank Schiffer, *Madras The Architectural Heritage* (Chennai: Indian National Trust For Art and Cultural Heritage Chennai Chapter 2003) p. 272.

THE TEMPLE OF THE LILY TANK

22 'Where are you Poompavai': S. Muthiah, *Madras Rediscovered* (Chennai: East West Press, 1999) p. 217.

22 'Mayura Sabda Pattinam': Ibid p. 216.

23 'The body of Messer': K. V. Raman, *The Early History of the Madras Region* (Chennai: Amudha Nilayam, 1959) p. 33.

24 'Mayilapur': Ibid., p. 29

24 'decoration': Ibid., p. 34

JOHN COMPANY FINDS A PLOT

27 'excellent long cloath': S. Muthiah, *Madras Rediscovered* (Chennai: East West Press, 1999) p. 2.

WHERE MODERN INDIA BEGAN

29 'the first Protestant': K. Kalpana and Frank Schiffer, *Madras The Architectural Heritage* (Chennai: Indian National Trust for Art and Cultural Heritage Chennai Chapter 2003) p. 51.

33 'I stand astonished': Michael Olmert, *Smithsonian* magazine, February 2001.

THE GOVERNORS CONSOLIDATE POWER

40 'murthered': S. Muthiah, *Madras Rediscovered* (Chennai: East West Press, 1999) pp. 16-17.

40 'not guilty': Ibid., p. 17.

42 'threatened the safety of': S. Anvar, 'Islam', *Madras: Chennai A 400-Year Record Of The First City Of Modern India—The Land, The People & Their Governance* (Chennai: Palaniappa Press, 2008) p. 21.

42 'four hundred bottles of liquors': Ibid., p. 121.

A GROWING DISCONTENT

47 'Considering what power': Rangaswami Parthasarathy, *A Hundred Years Of The Hindu* (Chennai : Kasturi and Sons Ltd., 1978) p. 48.

49 'It was salary day': N. Ramaswami Iyer, 'The Days With Bharathi', *The Hindu*, 18 October 1998.

COUNTERING CASTE HIERARCHIES

51 'the manifesto that': A. R. Venkatachalapathy, *Chennai Not Madras: Perspectives On The City* (Mumbai: Marg Publications, 2006) p. 5.

52 'had been equalled': Rangaswami Parthasarathy, *A Hundred Years Of The Hindu* (Chennai : Kasturi and Sons Ltd., 1978) p. 228.

52 'Long before the arrival': Ibid.

54 'The history of Chennai': A. R. Venkatachalapathy, *Chennai Not Madras Perspectives On The City* (Mumbai: Marg Publications, 2006) p.

55 'Despite the seeming': A. R. Venkatachalapathy, 'Madras Mannade', *Chennai Not Madras: Perspectives On The City* (Mumbai: Marg Publications, 2006) p. 18.

58 even as the Dravidian: A. Srivathsan, 'Politics, Architecture and the City', *Chennai Not Madras: Perspectives On The City* (Mumbai: Marg Publications, 2006) p. 50

58 'intelligently and dextrously': Ibid.

A LAYERED CITY

63 'Their story begins': Michel de Certeau, *The Practice of Everyday Life* translated by Stephen Rendell (Berkeley and Los Angeles: University of California Press, 1984) p. 98.

65 'Quinquireme of Nineveh': John Masefield, 'Cargoes', *The Nation's Favourite Poems* (London: BBC Books, 1996).

ENGA OORU—'OUR TOWN'

72 to the west of: S. Muthiah, *Madras Rediscovered* (Chennai: East West Press, 1999) p. 389.

73 how the library: Ibid pp. 391-392. Also see Henry Davison Love,

Vestiges of Old Madras 1640-1800 Vol. 1 (New Delhi: Mittal Publications, 1913) p. 215.

89 'we are all': Shashi Tharoor, 'Indian Identity is forged in diversity', *The Guardian*, 15 August 2007

OF PERFORMANCE AND SPECTACLE

98 'The devadasi's legacy': Lakshmi Vishwanathan, *Women of Pride: The Devadasi Heritage* (Chennai : Lotus Collection/ Roli Books, 2008) pp. 196-197.

110 'The development of': Stephen Hughes, 'Urban Mobility and the History of Cinema-Going in Chennai', *Chennai Not Madras: Perspectives On The City* (Mumbai: Marg Publications, 2006) p. 40.

110 the very first theatre: S. Muthiah, 'Cinema at Round Tana', *The Hindu*, June 25, 2003.

114 'among the 100': Richard Corliss and Richard Schickel, 'That Old Feeling: Secrets of the All Time 100', *Time*, 3 October 2011.

114 'replaced Leonardo': 'Dancing Maharajas', *Newsweek*, 9 May 1999.

CHENNAI AT LEISURE

117 'entered big cricket': Ramachandra Guha, 'Tamils and Turbans in Triplicane', *The Unhurried City: Writings on Chennai* (New Delhi Penguin Books India, 2004) pp. 103-104.

118 'stylish opening batsman': Soma Basu, '"I'm brutally frank": Krishnamachari Srikkanth', *The Hindu*, 14 September, 2012.

118 'swashbuckling': Partab Ramchand, ESPN cricinfo, September 2008.

118 'Four days of intense': Qamar Ahmed, 'A Befitting Climax', *The Hindu*, 1 February 1999.

119 'splendid': Ibid.

123 'educate' the people': A. Srivathsan, *Madras: The Architectural Heritage*, (Chennai: INTACH Tamil Nadu Chapter 2003) p. 51.

DEGREE COFFEE BY THE YARD

135 'the widespread use': A. R. Venkatachalapathy, *'Coffee-Drinking and Middle-Class Culture'*, *In Those Days There Was No Coffee—Writings in Cultural History—New Perspectives on Indian Pasts* (New Delhi: Yoda Press, 2006). p. 18.

137 'an initial cultural': Ibid., p. 14

137 'matched only by': Ibid.

139 '[Coffee] is not a habit': R. K. Narayan, *A Writer's Nightmare: Selected Essays 1958-1988*, (New Delhi: Penguin Books, 1988) pp. 55-56.

IN THE END, THE BEGINNING

145 'It is about': Gopalkrishna Gandhi, 'Chennai is us, its residents', *The Hindu*, 19 August 2012.

146 'Home is where': T.S. Eliot, 'East Coker', *Four Quartets: The Complete Poems and Plays 1909-1950* (New York: Harcourt Brace & World, Inc., 1952) p. 129.

BIBLIOGRAPHY

Ashokamitran, *Oru Paarvaiyal Chennai Nagaram* (Chennai: Kavitha Publications 2002).

a Bombay Walla, C. M., *Chutney Papers—Society, Shikar and Sport in India* (London: WH Beer & Co., Bombay: Thacker & Co. Limited 1984).

Ghosh, Biswanath, *Tamarind City—Where Modern India Began* (Chennai: Tranquebar Press 2012).

Hancock, Mary E., *The Politics of Heritage from Madras to Chennai* (Bloomington, Indiana: Indiana University Press 2008).

Kalpana, K. and Schiffer, Frank, *Madras: The Architectural Heritage* (Chennai: INTACH Tamil Nadu Chapter 2003).

Krishnan, Ramanathan and Krishnan, Ramesh, *A Touch of Tennis—The Story of A Tennis Family* (New Delhi: Penguin Books India, 2003)

Lakshmi, C. S. (Ed.), *The Unhurried City: Writings on Chennai* (New Delhi: Penguin Books India, 2004).

Love, Henry Davison, *Vestiges of Old Madras Indian Records Series*, Volumes 1-4 (New Delhi: Mittal Publications, 1995).

Madras Tercentenary Celebration Committee, *The Madras Tercentenary Commemoration Volume* (Madras: Humphrey Milford Oxford University Press, 1939).

Menon, Indira, *The Madras Quartet: Women in Karnatak Music* (New Delhi: Roli Books, 1999).

Muthiah, S., *Madras Rediscovered* (Chennai: East West Press, 1999).

Muthiah, S. *Madras that is Chennai—Gateway to the South* (Ranpar Publishers, 2005).

Muthiah, S. (Ed.)., *Madras (Chennai): A 400-year record of the First City of Modern India—The Land, The People & Their Governance* (Chennai: Palaniappa Brothers, 2008).

Muthiah, S. (Ed.)., *Madras (Chennai): A 400-year record of the First City of Modern India—Services, Education & The Economy* (Chennai: Palaniappa Brothers, 2012).

Nambi Arooran, K., *Tamil Renaissance and Dravidian Nationalism, 1905–1944* (Madurai: Koodal Publishers, 1980).

Narasimhan, V. K., *Builders of Modern India—Kasturi Ranga Iyengar* (New Delhi: Publication Division, Ministry of Information and Broadcasting, Government of India, 1963).

Narasimhan, V. K., *Kasturi Srinivasan* (Bombay: Popular Prakashan, 1969).

Narayan, R. K., *A Writer's Nightmare: Selected Essays, 1958–1988* (New Delhi: Penguin Books, 1988).

Narayan, R. K., *The Writerly Life: Selected Non-Fiction* (New Delhi: Penguin Books, 2001, 2002).

Pamuk, Orhan, *Istanbul: Memories and the City* (London: Faber and Faber Limited, 2005).

Pandian, M. S. S., Srivathsan, A. and Radhakrishnan, Mahesh, *Chennai: Museum, Exhibition, Backyard* (INTACH).

Parthasarathy, Rangaswami, *A Hundred Years of The Hindu* (Chennai: Kasturi & Sons Ltd., 1978).

Prakash, Gyan, *Mumbai Fables* (New Delhi: Harper Collins Publishers India, 2010).

Raban, Jonathan, *Soft City* (London: Harvill Press, 1998)

Raman, K. V., *The Early History of The Madras Region* (Chennai: The C. P. Ramaswami Aiyar Foundation, 2008).

Venkatachalapathy, A. R., *In Those Days There Was No Coffee—Writings in Cultural History—New Perspectives on Indian Pasts* (New Delhi: Yoda Press, 2006).

Venkatachalapathy, A. R. (Ed.), *Chennai Not Madras—Perspectives on the City* (Mumbai: Marg Publications, 2006).

White, E. B., *Here is New York* (New York: The Little Bookroom, 1976).

White, E. B., *Essays of E. B. White* (New York: Harper Perennial Modern Classics, 1999).

White, Edmund, *The Flaneur—A Stroll through the Paradoxes of Paris* (London: Bloomsbury, 2001, 2008).

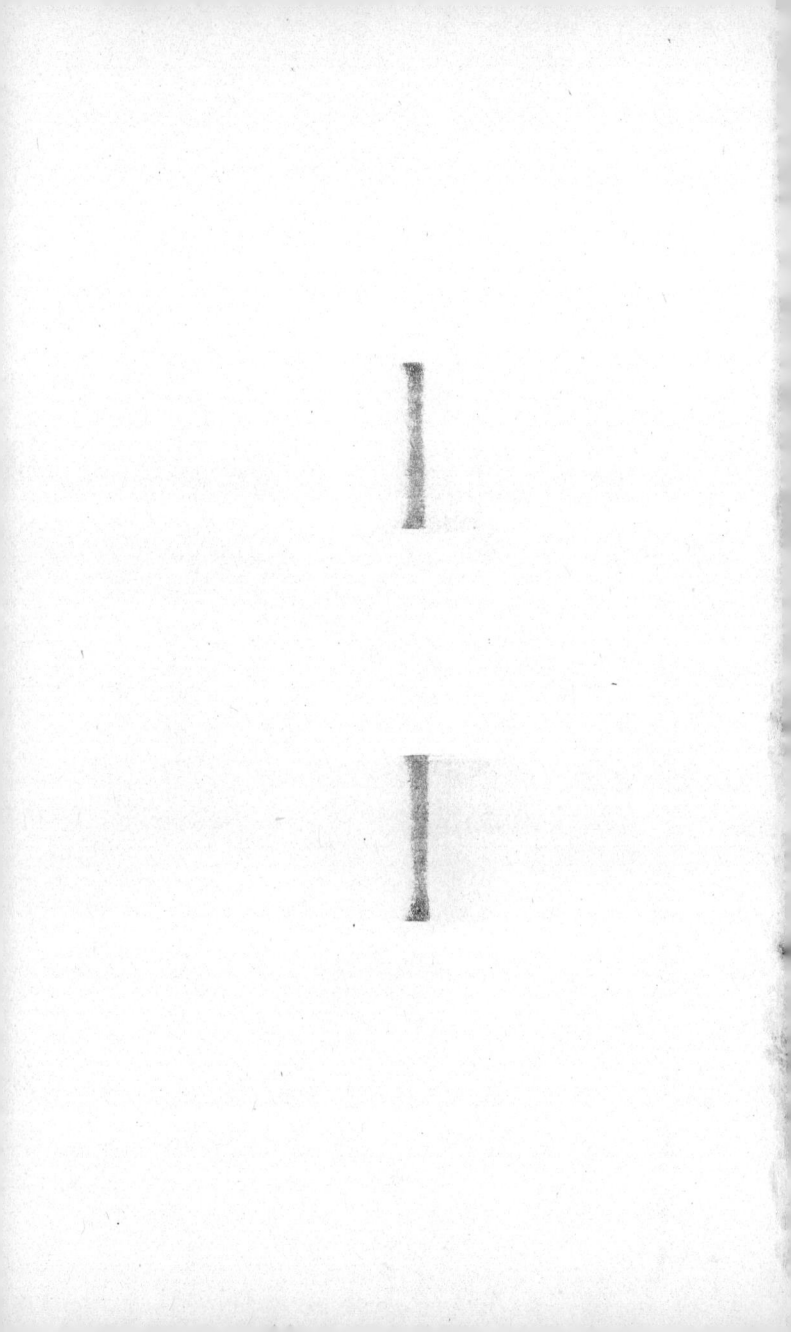